Debra

PURPOSEFUL
parenting

*Allowing God to Change Your Heart
so He Can Reach Theirs*

use your parenting power!

Tyra

TYRA LANE-KINGSLAND

Good Success Publishing

Purposeful Parenting
©2017 by Tia Lane-Kingsland

Requests for information should be addressed to:
Good Success Publishing, P.O. Box 5072, Upper Marlboro, MD 20775
ISBN 978-0-9978332-3-2

Library of Congress Control Number: 2017936002
This book is printed on acid-free paper

All scripture quotations, unless otherwise indicated, are taken from the
New International Version. Used by permission. All rights reserved.

Cover design: August Pride, LLC
Interior design: Adina Cucicov

Printed in the United States of America

dedication

*This book is dedicated to my sweet little flock.
What a treasure it is to walk alongside you on
this journey called life. Thank you for helping
me be a better human being. I pray God's
perfect will prevails in your lives today and
evermore. And I rejoice in the hope that the
seeds being planted today will reap a harvest
for generations to come.*

CONTENTS

Chapter 1

WHY ARE WE HERE?

*I will instruct you and teach you in the way
you should go; I will counsel you with my
eye upon you. Psalm 32:8*

I SAW A BABY ONESIE recently that said "The Snuggle Is Real". Aww, how cute. Yeah, the snuggle is real but so is the struggle. The job of parenting is not for the faint of heart. While the journey is filled with hugs, smiles and snuggles, it also comes with doubts, fear and worry. But no need to worry Friend, you are not alone. Single dads, I see you. Harried mama, I'm there with you. Educator, I respect you. Grandma, I honor you.

Have you ever asked yourself, "Am I doing the right thing for my kids?" Maybe you've prayed, "Lord I hope I'm not messing them up." The job of parenting can be laced with so much guilt and fear. Guilt that questions, "Am I doing enough?" Guilt that asks, "Am I doing too much hand holding?" Guilt that wonders, "Am I too hard on them?" Fear that asks, "Will they end up ok?" The thought of knowing you are holding someone's life in your hands and you just don't want to mess it up is a weighty matter.

If any of this rings true for you, let's celebrate because you've landed in the right place. We are knee deep in the trenches together, with compass in hand looking to point our children North. The challenge is that there is a difference between magnetic north and True North. Your best efforts may point them toward magnetic north. But God desires for them to head True North. And their True North is the plan and purpose God has destined for each of them since the foundation of the earth. Our plans for them may be good but God's plans for them are the BEST! And our job is to come into alignment with God as He carries out those plans.

Being a parent is not for cowards. It requires courage, resilience, and determination. It is a never-ending work that calls us to be proactive and diligent. Parents must be persistent in fighting for their children. And the fight takes place on our knees. Today's parent must have grit, keeping the long-range view before them while not getting lost in the minutia of what's happening today. Minute by minute, hour by hour and day by day you are making an investment in your children. And this investment will reap residual blessings that your great grandchildren will inherit. The hope in that makes my spirit leap for joy.

HOW DID YOU GET HERE?

Considering people have been rearing children since the dawn of humanity, one would think we'd have mastered parenting by now. But is there really a right way? We don't know for certain how they'll end up so we spin our wheels trying to ensure the best possible outcome. We carefully manufacture every facet of their lives right down to marching into the principal's office to demand the teacher of our choice. We want them to be "well-rounded" so they must play a sport, speak a foreign language, go on mission trips, and travel on competitive teams. Yup, I know all about it. You're not the only one. Been there, done that and wearing the t-shirt. But not only that; they must eat only organic, gluten free, and sugar free. So, dinner at Grandma's becomes a delicate dance as to not offend her. Friends, what are we *really* doing here?

I was having a conversation with a woman recently and she posed a very interesting thought. She said, and I quote, "People should learn how to become parents before they have children." Is that really possible? It made me think of preparing for childbirth. You can read about each month of pregnancy and what to expect. You can tour the hospital where you'll deliver. You can attend Lamaze classes, practice hypno-birthing or the Bradley Method, but when that first contraction hits, it's as if you've had no preparation at all. It can take your breath away. It sends most women into a panic screaming for an epidural.

Parenting is somewhat like that. You can read the parenting manuals. And believe me, there are plenty of them on the market.

You can read about gentle parenting, conscious parenting, helicopter parenting, free-range parenting, Christian parenting, and the list goes on. But until you come face-to-face with certain childhood situations, you don't know how you'll respond. Your own experiences as a child, your child's temperament, and your environment all play into how you will respond.

Looking among the droves of parenting books can leave you downright overwhelmed. There are books on raising socially adept, emotionally intelligent, sensory smart, highly-developed brained, cooperative, well-behaved, grateful, globally minded, happy, or healthy children. And our demands on our children can be downright overwhelming. We want them to get on the honor roll, have perfect attendance, be good stewards over the earth, minimize their carbon footprint, be model citizens, be quiet and obedient, and build their resumes. Whew! Poor kids. My heart goes out to you, my comrades, moving at break neck pace, all in an effort to raise children who will grow up to be successful adults.

I'm right here running alongside you. Though I'm beginning to slow the pace as I want to ensure all this movement is moving my children's hearts toward God, not away from Him. I'm trying to raise children whose hearts are open to give and receive love; children who will love God, love themselves and love others. With a heart that loves, I believe all those other things will fall into place. Yet the pressure is tremendous. While we may have the same amount or even more time with our children than parents had a century ago, how is that time being spent?

Parents are frenzied shuttling from school pick ups to soccer games then dropping the child's friend off then back again and eating fast food on the way because surely there's no time to sit at the table to eat and converse. All the while, your child has ear buds in, and you're not engaging one another in meaningful conversation. What's happening here?

I say it's time we reclaim parenting. We will not succumb to the pressure of what we think parenting ought to look like. We don't have to feel inadequate and then try to compensate by turning our children into productivity robots. Nope. We'll get back to loving and laughing, teaching and training. Remember parent, you are the heart mender, boo-boo healer, truth teller, attitude regulator, gift giver, confidant, playmate, coach, mentor and guide.

In our nation, we see children in crisis. The juvenile justice system is overrun with youth. As a result, many are even being sentenced as adults. Lawmakers are beginning to admit that the system is due for a complete overhaul.[1] Government and private industry are banking on our children ending up in the system, so preparations are being made for a booming prison population. It grieves my heart. I'm not saying that better parenting would cure every societal woe, but starting there would surely be a step in the right direction. What we need then are courageous parents who will claim their rightful position as shepherds, carefully tending their sheep. We need parents who will assume their position of authority and influence and carry it out in love.

Many factors may have contributed to you picking up this book. Maybe you yearn to make it peaceably through the day with your children. Maybe you just need a little encouragement. As you read these pages, I hope our hearts come into alignment with our desires for our children. I want children to know that we see them. I want them to know they are special, they matter and they are loved. Can you imagine for a moment how our world would change if each child knew and embraced that they are loved? What do you hope to see in the lives of the children in your circle of influence? What then will you do as an influencer to ensure all the children in your circle are affirmed?

In our role as parent, shepherd, and influencer, we lack the true metrics to know if we're doing it right. On the job, it's relatively easy to assess your performance. There, you would have been given a specific set of requirements and those requirements have metrics. Perhaps you are to increase revenue by a certain percentage, increase customer satisfaction, or reduce turnover. Not so with parenting. How can you ever truly measure whether or not your efforts have been successful?

Not to mention it's a job most people do with no training. On the job, you usually have new hire training, occasionally continuing education classes, leadership training, refresher courses and the like. Yet, parents are expected to learn on the job and master the role. We're expected to make it look easy and for our execution to be flawless. Others are watching and looking for the outcome. Some parents even use their children's achievements as a barometer of successful parenting. What school did your kid get into? What extracurricular activities are they involved in? And we begin seeing this in families with children that are still in pre-school!

Parenting is tough; no doubt about it. In fact, if most parents knew what they were really facing when becoming parents, they'd probably shy away from it. But there's no turning back now. If you're reading this book, you've probably got children or are serving in a parental role. Kudos to the few who are reading this in anticipation of becoming parents. Hopefully, reading this book won't scare you too much (insert emoji smile). But really, all jokes aside, this is a job that requires muscles. You can't be a parent and be weak. And I'm not talking physically strong or throwing your power around. I'm talking about the strength to tell your child, "I'm sorry." I'm talking about the strength to address behavior when you're dog-tired. I'm talking about the strength to exercise self-control when you want to yell. This requires a great deal of fortitude and selflessness.

There are no perfect parents. There is no magic formula. Do we ever really know what we're doing? I'm not sure. I would espouse we all want to go to bed at the end of the day with our children feeling loved and valued. We want to rest our heads knowing we've loved them well and that we did the best we knew how with the skill set we had at the time. Because let's face it, raising children has way too many variables and can carry us in many directions, which points to our need to trust only in the ONE who does know the exact coordinates. Trusting God is the only surety we have. For He knows our child's beginning from the end. In the process of us trying to figure it out, hopefully, we won't mess them up too bad. Just kidding. Well, sort of.

So, you do the best you can and hope for a great outcome. While we may not always know exactly what to do with and for our children, there are some things we can do on purpose that will reap a bountiful harvest. We can skillfully till the soil of our children's hearts, plant God's truth and trust the Holy Spirit to flow His rivers of living water, bringing about the increase.

HOW DID I GET HERE?
SIX CHILDREN.

"These are the children God has graciously given to me, your servant," Genesis 33:5

Who would have thought I'd be the mother of six? Not me. When I was a child, I had typical childhood fantasies of having a fine husband, driving a nice car and living in a big house. My parents were never married and of the families in my neighborhood, finding a married couple was like looking for a needle in a haystack. My vision of this perfect family included two kids, a boy and a girl, of course. (I don't even know where that "one boy and one girl makes a perfect family" thing began; and the fact that it still lingers today is even more perplexing as well-meaning family, friends, coworkers and even strangers commented after I had a daughter and then a son, "Well you've got your girl and your boy, so you're done right?" People say interesting things they don't really 'think' about. Excuse me for digressing.)

While being a parent is proving to be one of the most rewarding and fulfilling experiences I've ever had, it is by far the hardest thing I've ever done. For some, work may prove to be one of the most difficult things they've ever faced. I feel like, with a clear set of performance expectations coupled with my talent, knowledge, skill and ability, I can meet and even exceed an employer's expectations. Working a job, I can handle that.

For some, marriage may prove to be one of the most difficult things they've ever had to face. Joining forces with a person who may have different values, cares, likes, and interests or even a different upbringing can evoke trouble. How your spouse squeezes up the toothpaste or even something as simple as hanging up his or her towel (or lack thereof); the differences in marriage are not always easy to navigate. My husband and I met when we were freshmen in college so essentially we've grown up together. Through constant communication, we have been able to create a beautiful union and we look forward to growing old together. In marriage, when the expectations and roles are clearly defined and both parties have committed to executing their duties, marriage works.

For others, it may be dealing with a relative, an overbearing mother or an absent father. These familial relationships can bring about their own drama causing one to feel like being a relative is the hardest thing they've ever done. Employee. Wife.

Relative. I feel like those are roles I can execute with a pretty certain degree of success.

Parenting on the other hand…well, it is the hardest thing I have ever done.

"I know God won't give me anything I can't handle. I just wish he didn't trust me so much." Mother Teresa

What about you? Did you have preconceived notions before becoming a parent? Has the picture changed? Have you traded in rose-colored lenses for bifocals? If you are questioning your role as a parent, please don't discount the enormity of the role you play. You, my friend, are vital to the health and success of our world. You are your child's heart director. It is your responsibility to steer, direct and lead your children. And God sent them specifically to YOU. He believes in you. He's placed in you everything you need to shepherd them.

Parenting with purpose seeks to raise children who will actively contribute to making this planet a better place to live. That is a tremendous undertaking. The job becomes even more complex when you add in differences in genders, personalities, proclivities, likes, dislikes, and temperaments. But just as the African Peanut Stew I had for dinner last night was a mélange of vegetables, spices, beans and more, it came together to create magic on the tongue. The same can be said of our children. Their range of experiences will come together to help make this world better.

It is in being purposeful and intentional in learning each individual child and ministering to the heart of the child that the hard work ensues. It is the process of figuring out that my third born needs words of affirmation and my fourth born needs physical touch in order for them to truly feel loved that makes parenting a challenge. My children didn't carry a poster or verbally tell me, "Mommy, this is what I need". It took and continues to take careful observation and listening to discover who they are and what they need.

Parenting is the hardest thing when other children reject your child and part of you wants to go to the school seeking vengeance. Part of you may remember what it was like being rejected as a child and you may still be crippled by that thing; your own childhood trauma leaving you paralyzed, unable to help your child through their issues. It's the hardest thing when you know you've consistently taught them values such as caring, respect and honor and then they turn around and behave in a way completely opposite of what they've been taught. You may feel ashamed or embarrassed. But in the midst of the hard stands tall and erect—TRUTH. And the truth says:

"For I know the plans I have for you," declares the Lord, "plans to prosper you and not to harm you, plans to give you hope and a future." Jeremiah 29:11

So be encouraged! While parenting may be one of the hardest things you've ever done, it will reap a harvest for generations to come. And for your bobbles, stumbles and failures along the way, wear them as a badge of honor. It means that you showed up and are in the ring fighting on behalf of your children. You were called to this and didn't recoil in fear, but stepped up in faith.

Over the years, I've had people tell me parenting is my ministry. I heard it over and over again. I would cringe every time I heard it. Apparently, onlookers were seeing something I didn't see. I saw myself as a tightly wound mama precariously teetering on the edge of the precipice. Many days, I felt I would dive head first into the pit "PARENTING FAILURE". Each time I would yell at my children when I really didn't mean to or rushed them off to bed because I was tired and had had enough, I felt like I was failing.

But God! He has the ability to help us see ourselves as He sees us. He confirms our true identity in Him. Receive this truth: you are a good parent. Your bravery to accept children into your life, to give selflessly and even reading this book are all evidence of your love and commitment to the young people in your life.

THE KID CONUNDRUM

Who knew that getting children fed, dressed and out the door on time would be cause for celebration? And if it all happened without someone having a meltdown and that someone being me, well count it a magnificent day. Give me a high five somebody! Before having children, did you envision little people sitting at the dinner table quietly conversing? Could you have ever imagined then a kid dunking two hands into a jar of Nutella and then proceeding to smear them on your white walls? Parenting is quite a mystery but God seeks to make the mysteries known to us. He wants to take the guesswork out of it.

While your home may not be immaculate enough to warrant a photo shoot in Better Homes and Gardens, and your meals may not be 100% organic and your child may embarrass you at church by throwing a temper tantrum, you can still create a home life that is filled with love. Joy in parenting can be your portion. Imagine little arms and legs stretched out on throw blankets all over the family room floor, teen siblings curled up on the couch sharing secrets, and a child on your lap, all glimpses of the love, joy and security found in the home life you've created. When God has given you an assignment, He'll give wisdom, resources and grace to carry it out. I say, "If God calls you to it, He'll give you grace to do it!" Parenting requires holy insight and God is faithful to grant it to us. We simply have to ask.

"Ask, and it will be given to you; seek, and you will find; knock, and it will be opened to you. For everyone who asks receives, and the one who seeks finds, and to the one who knocks it will be opened. Or which one of you, if his son asks him for bread, will give him a stone? Or if he asks for a fish, will give him a serpent? If you then, who are evil, know how to give good gifts to your children, how much more will your Father who is in heaven give good things to those who ask him!"
Matthew 7:7-11

Perhaps your coming to this book was your way of asking. Let us incline our ear then and hear what God has to say. He is the Good Shepherd and will lead us in paths of righteousness for his namesake. He wants to give us good gifts and he's done so in gifting us with children. Psalm 127:3 says, *"Children are a heritage, offspring a reward from him"*. Not only has he blessed you but He's also equipped you for a time such as this.

SO, WHAT ARE WE TO DO?

Raising whole children starts with being a whole parent. And by whole, I mean feeling complete; loved physically, spiritually, socially and emotionally. To raise a whole child you must first raise yourself. This became painfully apparent to me as I examined my interactions with my children. There were times in parenting that I found myself over- reacting or overly emotional. My responses were not commensurate with the things my children had done. I knew something was off but I couldn't quite place it.

God showed me that, as I child, I had adopted a negative core belief and was parenting through that belief. I adopted a negative core belief that I was unworthy thus, unlovable. This showed up in my interactions with my children as *over* parenting. Because of this belief, my children would *know* that I was in charge, that I was the parent, and that I was in control. I was parenting from this place of brokenness. I embarked on a healing journey and God uprooted that negative core belief among other areas of hurt.

If you feel something underlying is impacting your parenting, pray and ask God to reveal it to you. Once He reveals it, the gateway is open for healing. Reveal then heal, that's how He works. So starting with self is the beginning. And because God wants you to be in health and prosper as your soul prospers (3 John 1:2), He is faithful to do it.

This journey then is not some "Twelve Steps to Get Your Kid Right" strategy. Nor is it some New Age parenting methodology. What I am sharing are nuggets that I've mined over nearly two decades of tapping into the little hearts of my beloved: my sister whom I raised from early teens to adulthood, my own six children and countless other little people along the way. I've practiced, refined and tailored this information as my own household has grown and in coaching countless parents through classes and workshops.

How do we do it? How do we raise children that are compassionate and considerate, loving and kind, world changers yet humble? It is no easy task. Meeting a child's spiritual, physical, social, emotional, and mental needs calls for a multi-pronged approach that is grounded in Christ. We may have to ditch some commonly held parenting advice and instead rely on the Holy Spirit's guidance. We may have to block out the naysayers. We will be required to look deeply into our children's hearts and see their fragility, see their vulnerability and protect their innocence. We will have to show up, and make ourselves available physically, mentally and emotionally knowing that our children look to us for love, compassion, understanding, comfort, and protection.

We are raising the child that would grow up to be the type of boss that we'd want to work for. We are rearing a child that will grow up to be the type of Pastor we'd sit under, or the type of spouse we'd want for one of our children. Our aim is to fill them with love until they overflow so that they then pour that love unto God, themselves and others. Does this require you to be the perfect parent? No. There's no such thing. In fact, every day I'm learning on the job and I bet you are too. And while there are no perfect parents, we serve a perfect God who will work mightily through us in our parenting.

When I set out to write this book, I thought I would give a pretty clinical discourse on raising children. I thought I would share some of the leading research on child rearing. But you know what? That information is easy to come by. Do you really need more information? The Bible says in Revelation 12:11, "*They triumphed over him by the blood of the Lamb and by the word of their testimony.*" It is in the sharing of stories, in seeing others in action and trial and error experiences that we learn. So, that's what we've got here. I'm sharing from my personal experiences, but also from what I've witnessed in others' experiences. From families parenting one child to another parenting ten. From families that believe in spanking to those that utilize only a gentle approach. Whether parenting children with high needs or managing crazy family calendars, in all our experiences, some basic truths emerge. I have attempted to capture them and present them here.

Like Moses approaching Pharaoh, you may feel somewhat inadequate in your role as a parent. God specializes in using our inadequacies to do great works for Him. Just as the Lord provided Moses with reassurance and backing from the great I AM, He still IS and will always BE with you. It is from the place of inadequacy or not knowing, that God can do some of His greatest work. From this place of questioning, you tend to spend more time in God's word, pray more fervently and seek Him for solutions. Yes, parenting is one of those areas that will keep you clinging fiercely to the old rugged cross.

When approaching any new material, it can be overwhelming to process then apply all you've read. It is my prayer that as you read this book, the nuggets of truth will grip your heart. As they do, I pray you will meditate on that truth and ask the Lord how He would have you apply it with the young people in your life. Commit the foundational verses located at the start of each chapter to memory. Go back and read the closing prayers frequently. And give the practical application your best effort.

As you move through these pages, it is my prayer that you will be inspired to love long and love strong. On the hard-parenting days, may the words in this book trigger you to choose well. May you choose to hug when you want to scold, may you choose to listen when you want to yell and choose love above all because indeed love does cover a multitude of sins. God has trusted us enough to place the blessing of children in our hands. Let us honor God by carefully nurturing His treasured posses- sion, His children. Let us be filled with compassion. Let us see them as He sees them. Let us be filled with hope and stand fast to His promises.

And if you feel you've missed the mark, it's okay. Every day for me isn't a homerun. Some days I feel like an epic fail and I desperately want a do over. Yet, in the midst of the failed attempts, Jesus is still there. He extends His hand of grace. He forgives, nurses our wounds and gives us another opportunity to get it right. He confirms that even when we make parenting mistakes, He still loves us. He gives us children whose hearts are loving, receptive and forgiving.

Parenting is not a sprint but a decathlon. So, on days when troubles are long and patience is short, let's remember the big picture. Generations to come will be impacted by the seeds of love you are sowing into your children today. We are not in this for the quick win but for the generational victory. It is my prayer that you will leave this book inspired, motivated and challenged. I pray you will be filled with more love, more compassion and more grace. I hope this book serves as an answer to your prayers. You can do this! So, let's get to work then!

Starting here and concluding every chapter, I challenge you to DO the practical application. We will also pray together. The word of God assures us that where two or three are gathered in His name He will be in the midst (Matthew 18:20). Well, we are joined through these pages so He's right here with us. That's good news!

PRACTICAL APPLICATION

1. Pray and ask God to reveal any areas of hurt from your own past. Journal any revelation and pray for healing.

2. If your child is of age, let them know you are reading this book. Share with them you are always learning and growing and that includes being a parent. Apologize if necessary and let them know how excited you are that God's chosen you to be their parent.

prayer

*Lord, what an honor it is to shepherd the flock
entrusted into my care. Thank you for calling
me to this esteemed position of parent, mentor,
teacher, coach and influencer. I confess that
I don't always get it right. Lord, I repent for
times in parenting when I haven't listened to
your voice and have tried to do it my way. You
said ask and I shall receive, so I'm asking for
divine wisdom on how to raise children that
will love you, love themselves and serve their
community. Your word affirms that you gently
lead those with young. Thank You for your
gracious guidance, direction and redirection as
I walk out the high calling of parenting.*

⤙

Chapter 2

GOD'S PLAN AND PURPOSE

*"That the generation to come might know
them (God's commands), The children who
would be born, That they may arise and
declare them to their children, That they may
set their hope in God, And not forget the
works of God, but keep His commandments."
Psalm 78:6-7*

BEFORE WE EVEN ATTEMPT TALKING parenting strategies,
let's place the family in its proper context. Children are key
members of the family and the family unit is near to the heart
of God. Jesus himself was born into a family. Considering He is
divine, He could have simply materialized on earth but it didn't
happen that way. He was born of the womb and nestled into the

loving secure environment of the family. If God uses families in this way, they must be a powerful force on the earth. And since children are the nucleus of family life, they must be special to God. We have evidence of God's heart toward children. "*People were bringing little children to Jesus for him to place his hands on them, but the disciples rebuked them. When Jesus saw this, he was indignant. He said to them, "Let the little children come to me, and do not hinder them, for the kingdom of God belongs to such as these. Truly I tell you, anyone who will not receive the kingdom of God like a little child will never enter it." And he took the children in his arms, placed his hands on them and blessed them." Mark 10:13-16* Jesus welcomed the children to himself, He held them and He blessed them. Indeed, children are special to God.

When in the full throws of the day-to-day parenting grind, it is easy to lose sight of the bigger picture. It is easy to forget how special our children are to God and the significant role they play in His kingdom. For that reason, we have to be intentional about keeping an eternal mindset. It is God's ultimate desire that your children and their children know Him and place their hope in Him. While the everyday affairs of parenting may seem important in the moment, God's plans and purposes for your child and mine are great. For that reason, we must continually keep the end in mind.

In one of the best-selling management books ever, *The 7 Habits of Highly Effective People*, Stephen Covey shares wisdom on how to achieve both personal and professional effectiveness. Habit #2 is "Begin With The End In Mind". I put forth that achieving both joyous children and sane parents, requires one to begin with the end in mind. If not, the first few months of parenting could leave you questioning your ability to effectively care for a little human. Who knowingly signs up for sleepless nights, constant diaper changes, and failing at interpreting cries? But the end in mind says, this is just a season. Before I know it, they'll be talking and heading to Kindergarten so let me embrace this time. It takes the end in mind to not give up, knowing "homework tears" don't last always. With the end in mind, you see your young scholar in her cap and gown on graduation day.

Are you making today's decisions with tomorrow in mind? When arranging your family's priorities and forming your habits, are you doing so with the next generation in mind? When I think of the level of work that's involved in each of our complicated lives, my ready answer is that, most often, we aren't making decisions with the end in mind. Heck! We are just trying to make decisions that will help us make it to bedtime successfully!

Beginning with the end in mind enables us to not get lost in the minutiae of child-rearing. When we keep an eternal focus, we don't allow little things to dissuade us. With the end in mind, our children's behavior doesn't become a distraction; it just becomes a prompt for prayer. With an eternal perspective, that unruly kid our child has chosen to befriend is seen as our child leading their friend in paths of righteousness for His namesake. The end in mind frees us to see the stubborn child not as obstinate but as one who will stand firm in his convictions for Christ. And with our eye set on destiny, we see them as

Christ sees them and He sees a future and a hope. He sees good and not evil. He sees what He's planned before the foundation of the Earth. And in His sight, it is good. An eternal mindset frees you to love. And love sees potential. Love sees purpose. Love sees destiny fulfilled. Will you keep the end in mind and come into His line of sight so you can see what He sees?

> *"Do not grow weary in doing good for in due season you will reap a harvest IF you do not give up!" Galatians 6:9*

GOD'S DESIGN FOR THE FAMILY

> *"So God created mankind in his own image, in the image of God he created them; male and female he created them. God blessed them and said to them, 'Be fruitful and increase in number; fill the earth and subdue it. Rule over the fish in the sea and the birds in the sky and over every living creature that moves on the ground.'" Genesis 1:27-28*

From Genesis on, we see that God moves with deliberate order and purpose. He systematically created everything under the heavens in divine order to serve a specific purpose. And a significant part of His orderly design was the creation of the family. Today, we see personal choices, societal and cultural norms attempting to distort His design, but the design doesn't change. Just as a hammer is designed to bang in nails or pull them out, His design serves a purpose. If we decide to use a hammer to bust through drywall or if we decide to use our shoe in place of the hammer, that does not negate the hammer's intended purpose, which is to place or remove nails. Even if you decide to use a hammer with a screw and not a nail, the hammer is still a hammer. The screw is out of place, not the hammer.

So, what has happened to the family structure God designed? It's been modified and like the hammer, not always being used as intended. The media has reduced the role of father to a buffoon or portrays him as absentee. But I beg to differ. The last time I went to the playground in fact, I saw MORE children with fathers than I did with mothers. It is my husband that engages with the children in their science club and it is the fathers that are teaching the classes. It is the fathers I see involved with hundreds of scouts on a weekly basis. It is the fathers I see helping direct traffic in the school parking lot. While mother and father were together with their son, it was the father I saw stoop to explain the color variation in the layers of limestone. But the fathers are also under a great deal of stress trying to find the elusive work/life balance.

Our culture today does not esteem the role of mother either. In fact, the role has been demonized. We've even gone so far as to indoctrinate children through many popular animated films that the role of mother is unnecessary. Mother has systematically been erased from these films or is represented as an evil figure. Young women are encouraged to put off being a mother for as long as possible. They are encouraged to pursue career and travel over family. I can recall a birth control commercial where four women go shopping together. In the store, they pick up college degrees, men, travel, and a home. The stork dangles a baby, beckoning one of the women to come closer. She stops, turns toward the stork, puts a hand up and mouths "No Thank You." This is a pretty accurate depiction of what we see playing out in the world today. Then when the working woman does have children, oftentimes, she spends long hours outside the home while the children are away from home at aftercare and/ or attending multiple extra-curricular activities.

And while we are at it, where are the grandparents? Some are retirement age, but feel pressured to continue working so that they are not a burden to their adult children. Because their children have relocated, they are sometimes hundreds of miles away from their grandchildren. Grandparents directly impact a child's values and beliefs. The rich wisdom that grandparents dispense is hampered when grandparents have limited opportunity to connect with their grandchildren. The grandparent-child bond is one that cannot be matched. The grandparent serves as historian, mentor, guru, protector and playmate. In many of today's families, this role is sorely missed.

I would like to add just one additional key member of family life—the teacher. In fact, your child's teacher may spend even more direct time with your child than you do. But even the role of teacher has changed. In some cases, you find teachers whose main reason for teaching is to pay off their student loans not so much their passion for shaping young minds. Then, those teachers that actually care are being restricted from their level of involvement. Gone are the days when teachers are free to give their students hugs. Gone are the days when teachers can mediate a disagreement between two students they know very well as they're required to refer the students to the guidance counselor. Loving and caring teachers, I see you and I appreciate your contribution! You offer stability that helps keep children grounded when family life may be topsy-turvy.

While many of these changes to the family structure are not inherently wrong, they alter the dynamics of the family. Those interruptions then run over and are seen in the culture. The culture then is fragmented and broken. Finally, you end up with a society that is fractured. So where does this leave our children? They run the risk of living a good life albeit different than the excellent life God had prepared for them. They can potentially miss out on their rich inheritance. Will we be courageous enough to embrace God's original design for the family? The speed at which the kingdom advances hinges on our obedience. Will you align with His design?

It is also through the design of the family that God dispenses blessing. It is God's desire to not only bless you but for blessings to follow you, generation after generation. He wants your great-grandchildren to be recipients of blessings that were attached to your obedience. God says:

- Blessed is the man whose quiver is full (Psalm 127:5).
- He will love you, bless you, and multiply you; in the land he swore to your fathers he will give you (Deuteronomy 7:13).

- Children are a blessing and a reward (Psalm 127:3).
- Her children rise up and call her blessed (Proverbs 31:28).
- He will bless you and make your descendants as numerous as the stars in the sky and the sand on the shore (Genesis 22:17).

The blessings mentioned above are conditional and the condition is obedience. God's blessings <u>always</u> require obedience. Along your parenting journey, God will require you to make decisions that may be contrary to what you want to do. As we progress through these chapters, God will give you an opportunity to participate in living out his design for the family. Are you willing to completely obey God, knowing that your children's children will be a direct beneficiaries of the decisions you are making today?

GOD'S PLAN FOR YOUR CHILDREN

The very first blessing verbally communicated to man was, "*God blessed them and said to them, 'Be fruitful and increase in number; fill the earth and subdue it." Genesis 1:28* From this, we can deduce that it is God's desire to bless you through your seed. All potential is found in the seed. From a small seed, a sequoia tree can grow 30 feet in diameter to 250 feet tall. The sequoia is but a small illustration of the grand plans God has for your seed. Life is in the seed. Promise is contained within the seed. The enemy seeks to kill, steal and destroy the seed because he knows that's where the promise lies. But God's plans for your children, your seed, are blessings not curses to give them a future and a hope. While some seeds lie dormant and others have varying times of germination, the potential is there. Cloaked in a thin protective coating or behind the hard wall of stone fruit, greatness is there. Don't overlook the power of your seed. Don't forget to keep that eternal mindset. The end in mind always sees the potential in the seed. When you look upon your children, remember the sequoia. Your seeds are filled with hope and promise.

Your seed is not just the byproduct of a chance encounter between a man and a woman. Every single child that is created represents an intentional miracle performed by God. Since God knew each one before the foundation of the Earth, a child's birth serves a vital role in God's kingdom-building agenda. God says in Jeremiah 1:5, *"Before I formed you in the womb I knew you, before you were born I set you apart; I appointed you as a prophet to the nations."* God desires for that child to become an active citizen in the kingdom here on earth. And the family is a primary means through which God communicates and furthers the expansion of that kingdom.

Your children are a direct representation of God's handiwork. They are His workmanship and He created them with purpose on purpose. Let's celebrate and cultivate the fearfully wonderfully made persons God ordained for them to be.

"I thought that one day I would be a famous artist and create great works of art. Instead, God made me a mother, and my children are His masterpiece. The design

of their lives will live on after me. What is painted on their
hearts will last an eternity." Anonymous

Yes. God is the artist and your children are His masterpieces. As a parent, you can find yourself trying to be the artist. If you're not careful, you can find yourself skillfully trying to mold and construct these little humans into who you want them to be. Your artistry says the child has to appear perfect to onlookers. Your artistry says, "Be obedient and compliant. Sit quietly and keep still. Answer questions with enthusiasm when asked." Your artistry says, "Keep your clothes clean, chew with your mouth closed, and use your manners, for heaven's sake. You've got good home training!"

But what does it look like when The Master Artisan paints your children each with unique personalities and proclivities? It's more Picasso than Da Vinci, more abstract and theoretical than realistic and literal. It's your little one who runs across the table in Sunday school class. It's your child who rocks left to right or front to back repeatedly. It's your child who'd rather talk to bugs and trees than to people. It's your child with the incessant chatter.

As I stood at the window watching fat juicy snowflakes fall one night, I thought of the intricate detail in which they are fashioned. Their complex design emerges as they travel through different temperatures and humidity levels. God controls each and every part of the snowflake's formation and knows what the end design will be. Not too different from what happens to your children. He knew them before He knit them in the womb. Being born into their specific families, geographic location, race, and decade they are shaped and fashioned into intricate, complex human beings, created for accomplishing God's good works.

"For we are His workmanship, created in Christ Jesus for good works, which God prepared beforehand that we should walk in them." Ephesians 2:10

So, free yourself and your children by allowing them to be who they were created to be. Despite what you may think, God didn't create them to be your clones or mini-Me. He created them to be individual expressions of Himself since they are created in HIS image—not yours. OUCH! This truth stung me a bit too. He wants your children on display for all to see so that others may be drawn to Him.

God created each child with their own tendencies, likes, interests, and abilities. We have to love them for who they are. Accept them for who they are. Again, they are His work of art, not ours. We are to embrace and cultivate how God made them, and not try to force a square peg into a small circle. I was chatting with my neighbor about how well-meaning adults can adversely affect children by making them be something they are not. My neighbor vividly recalled the nuns at his Methodist primary school lashing his hand with a wooden ruler because he would write with his left hand. Repeatedly, he was disciplined for writing with the "wrong" hand. When forced to write with the right hand, his penmanship was deemed unacceptable and he was held back a grade. When he left that school, he was moved back up a grade. But the damage had already been done. From that early age, my neighbor was made to feel as if he was defective. He was made to feel his natural way of being was wrong.

What will be the long-term effects of trying to force a child to do or be something they simply are not? What is the benefit of trying to break someone out of the way they were fashioned? Parents, let us be sensitive to who God created our children to be and cultivate an environment conducive for their growth. We'll spend the next two chapters discussing how to connect with them in ways they can perceive and receive.

God's plans for them are exceedingly, abundantly above anything we can think or imagine. His plans for them are good. His plans cause everything to work out for their good even when our eyes deceive us and paint a different picture. So, let's be mindful to not overstep our bounds and trample upon the Artists' creation. While we do not want to be lax in our role as curators, let us trust the Artisan because He has the Master Plans.

THE PARENTAL ROLE

You know the airline saying, "In the event of an emergency, put your own oxygen mask on first"? As mentioned in the previous chapter, parenting requires us to do some soul searching. Interacting with your children has a way of putting your beliefs, attitudes, and behavior under a microscope. Under closer examination, do you like what you see? Even if the reflection is unfamiliar, it provides an opportunity for self-improvement. In order for you to lead anyone, you have to be rooted and grounded in who you are.

Christ equips you to know the way, go the way, and show the way to your children. While his expectations of you are high, He will faithfully walk hand in hand with you on your parenting journey. You just have to abide in Him. Here are two nuggets for you to hold on to.

GRACE

In parenting, you WILL make mistakes. It's just par for the course. Knowing that, be mindful to be gentle with yourself. Just as you aim to be gentle with your children, you owe it to yourself to be gentle with YOU. That means forgiving yourself when you make a mistake. It means not being overly critical of yourself. It means cancelling negative self-talk. It means not continually playing the recording of, *"I'm a horrible parent. Oh, I'll never get it right"*. Stop it! Simply do your best. When you've sinned against your child, repent to the Lord and apologize to your child. Rest in God's grace. Grace is God's unmerited favor. He gives to you an extra measure of love, kindness and gentleness, even if you feel you're undeserving.

One day, I had a mommy meltdown. I felt as if my children weren't doing anything I asked. I questioned how I had failed as a parent. As I sat on the side of my bed with my head hanging low, the Lord called out to me and told me to grab my bible. He said, *"Turn to Isaiah 54:13".* Now this has only happened to me one other time where God has literally grabbed me, sat me down and told me to turn to a specific, unfamiliar verse to address an immediate concern. And this is what it says, *"All your children will be taught by the Lord, and great will be their peace." Isaiah 54:13*

In that moment, God confirmed for me that despite how inadequate I felt as a parent, it is HE that is ultimately parenting my children. In that He gave me the reassurance that I am not alone on this journey as He is walking with me, helping me to parent each and every day. Isn't God amazing? He is so perfect. He is so timely. My encounter with God that day left an indelible impression on my heart. Now I can face each parenting day with confidence, knowing that He is right alongside me teaching my children.

VULNERABILITY

Your chest has been cracked wide open and your heart is exposed. Parenting is one of the GREATEST areas of vulnerability. You are wired to be fiercely protective of your little one lest they die. Long-tailed macaques will risk their lives fending off much larger animals to protect their babies. With your heart wide open, this vulnerability leaves you open and prone to attack or be attacked. We nitpick at how we see ourselves and are judgmental of other parents.

It's time to stop looking through the microscope of judgment and start seeing through the eyes of love and compassion. We have to be less critical of ourselves and of other parents. We are all in this together, equally muddy as we traverse knee deep in the trenches of parenting. We are all carrying a huge weight to keep them safe, healthy, spiritually grounded, sociable, educated, and disciplined. Whew! And if you feel you've failed any one of those, shame says, *"You're a terrible parent."* Well, I've come to reveal my heart. I am vulnerable and I expose the shame. None of us is perfect. I'm not judging you. In fact, I'm here to lend a hand. I'm not critical of your child in here with a runny nose. I'm not thinking, *"Won't you get him out of here?"* I'm looking at you because I want to know if you'll let me hold your sick baby while you tend to your other children. I see you because I *am* you.

WITH PURPOSE ON PURPOSE

The parental role is one of great purpose. As such, parenting is not something we just do on the fly nor is it something we do just because that's the way our parents did it with us. *"Well, we were raised that way and we turned out ok,"* some may think. While that may be the case, I'd like for my children to receive from me what God has called me to deliver and that calls for me to parent with purpose. I surrender parenting the way that is convenient or parenting in a way that's familiar but parenting the way God instructs.

Parenting this way requires wisdom and understanding. Again, this is the surety we have in Him. If we ask, He is faithful to deliver. He invites us to ask for wisdom and understanding (Proverbs 2:2-3). Through His precepts, we gain understanding

(Psalm 119:104). He feeds us with knowledge and understanding (Jeremiah 3:15). He duly equips us for the job at hand.

So, what are some of the parental duties? God has called you to nurture. Mothers, the Bible says that Sarah, Hannah, and Jochebed nursed their babies. Their children were held close as Mother provided life-sustaining nourishment. Though you may not have a baby at the breast, what are you doing to nourish your children mentally, physically and spiritually? And speaking of Jochebed, Moses' mother hid her son to protect him. Parents, we have a responsibility to hide our children under the shadow of the Almighty. When Herod was on the warpath killing little boys, Mary and Joseph fled to Egypt to hide Jesus. In what ways are you protecting your children from the evils of this world?

Parents also provide for their children. Every year, Hannah would return with a new robe for her son Samuel. This one, providing temporal needs, seems to be the area we spend the most energy on. While meeting temporal needs is important, it is not all- encompassing. Our culture has reduced parenting to simply providing care; food, clothing, shelter and when the child turns 18, they are out of your house. My hope is that we adopt a God-centered view of provision that doesn't cut them off at an assigned age. How about the spiritual growth of your children? Eunice and Lois provided spiritual training for Timothy.

Parents are called to provide guidance. This is an area we sometimes overstep our bounds. Guidance does not mean doing everything for them. Are you doing your child a service or a disservice in completing their homework for them? Teachers, can I get an Amen?! When she could no longer hide him, Jochebed put Moses in a carefully constructed vessel and placed her daughter in position to look over him. She guided him along a stream of living water. To guide is to lead or facilitate, but not to do everything for. Are there some areas where you need to remove your hands and just serve as a guide?

Parents, when facing fear, we will stand in faith. We will recall the Lord's promises to us regarding our children. Elizabeth said "NO!" to the naysayers and spoke up as to what the Lord told her about the child's name. She knew people wouldn't understand, but she didn't let that intimidate her. When the Lord makes a promise to you about one of your children, later for the naysayers. Continue to follow the Lord. Mary told the angel let it be to me as you have stated even though she'd risk persecution from the community and rejection from Joseph. In faith, continue to stand on God's promises for your children.

HOME LIFE

The home is the central nervous system of the family. In the home, children find a safe haven free from the pressure of the outside world. The home is a strong tower where your children are kept safe. Our job is to create an atmosphere at home that is nurturing, supportive and conducive for learning but also safe for making mistakes. Outside of doing homework, how much instruction is being done in the home? (Shout out to my homeschooling families. God sees you.) Are you teaching children how to cook and how to budget? Are you teaching how to change a flat tire or how to put a desk together?

There was a time when the home was the hub of all activity. From work to church, it all took place within or in very close proximity to the home. There was a time when husbands could come home in the middle of the day to have lunch. Those days have given way to families being out of the house more hours than they are in them. Dads, when you're at home, are you connecting with your family or taking refuge in your man cave? Moms, you've been called to be discreet, chaste, keepers of the home. But how can you "keep" your home if you spend so little time there?

The home as the central nervous system should give a constant relay of joy. Just as the central nervous system influences nearly every part of the body, joy should be seen and felt in every aspect of home life. Be reminded that in HIS presence there is fullness of joy. Just as His glory filled the temple, His glory can saturate your home. The joy-filled home washes away worry, flushes out tension and casts out fear. The joy-filled home invites cheer, laughter and smiles. Light a candle, play some music and bring in the joy.

So, how do we create joy-filled homes? Let's start by slowing down. How can we embrace joy when we are frenetically doing life "In-Between"? It seems that we do so much life in-between; shuttling our children from one activity to the next to the next. "Hurry up and get dressed!" "Hurry up and eat!" "Hurry up! We've gotta go!" "Hurry up so I can get you to soccer practice!" "Hurry up and do your homework!" "Hurry up and eat dinner!" "Hurry up and get to bed!" How can we experience joy at home when so much of life is just moving to the next thing on the schedule?

We have to be proactive in reclaiming time. We have to seize moments and make the most of them. Parents, create time in your children's schedule for them to move at a more relaxed pace. In my house, my husband wakes up the children earlier than they really need to so they don't feel rushed. In the afternoons, I've created a pocket of time for the children to spend outdoors so they can decompress from the intensity of the school day. And summer 2016, I did something really radical. I, the consummate planner, made no plans. I gave the children early notice that summer 2016 would be one like they'd never experienced before. Gone would be shuttling kiddos to a bunch of different camps, programs, and events and in would be relaxing days spent at home. And sure enough, that's just what we did. And, boy, did I enjoy being home! (It took having a newborn, baby #6, for me to get this revelation). It was such confirmation at the end of the summer when my firstborn told me it was the best summer ever. Why? Because we basically did nothing. Were they bored? Nope. Relaxed? Yes!

Parents, your role is invaluable. The health of our society is directly impacted by the work you are doing to parent on purpose with purpose. This job requires diligence, grit and determination. You may cry many tears, you may experience many sleepless nights, and you may become acquainted with inconvenience but it will all be worth it because Jesus sees your efforts in tending to your flock and He's poised to say, "Well Done!"

PASSIVE PARENTING

I would be remiss if I didn't address the opposite of purposeful parenting, which is passive parenting. Two years ago, at a women's conference at my church, I had an opportunity to meet Alicia Walls. She is "mama extraordinaire" of eight children and four of those eight are a popular gospel group, The Walls Group. So, I asked this mama, "Please, give me some nuggets of truth. Tell me how you do it {parenting}." She said, "Who you need to talk to is Mama Harper." Mama Harper is mother of Contemporary Christian artist Jamie Grace. So, Mama Walls proceeds to bring Mama Harper over to me. One look at Mama Harper and I know she's about to drop some knowledge on me. She immediately struck me as a sweet grandma type yet, a "take no mess" schoolteacher. She got right in my face, I mean ALL up in my face in her Zena Warrior Princess stance and asked me, "Are you a passive parent?" I paused for a moment, and replied no. Surely, I don't think of myself as passive in any way, shape or form. She asked me again a second time to which I again answered no.

She proceeded to challenge me with several parent/child scenarios after which she told me flat out, "You're Passive." She went on to command me not to be passive. It was a moment I'll never forget. As I reflected on our conversation over the next few weeks, I began to notice some of the truth she shared playing out. I did have occurrences of passive parenting.

Passive parenting lets the child play video games far too long because you're tired and you don't want to be bothered. Passive parenting sees a teen text something inappropriate but doesn't address it because you want to keep the peace. Passive parenting overlooks repeated misbehavior because, "Hey I've got my own real adult problems to deal with so I've got no time to help you work through yours".

Let me put it plainly. We cannot afford to be lazy or passive parents. Even when it is uncomfortable, we have to proactively parent. Just as we'll proactively plan a vacation, we must proactively engage with our children. I mean, who's really sitting around waiting with baited breath to talk about appropriate and inappropriate touch? I know, proactive parenting isn't always easy or convenient. Delving into a conversation with your child about police brutality isn't exactly light banter. Nope; proactive parenting is not easy but it's necessary. It will allow us to lay a foundation of truth. Then, any information our children receive thereafter has to be filtered through the truth that they've received from us, versus the other way around.

The duties of shepherds are tremendous. They are responsible for the welfare and safety of their flock. They tend to work around the clock providing care. They lead the flock to green pastures where grazing is plentiful. The flock is kept safe from all manner of wildlife: wolves, coyotes, bears and mountain lions. They are kept close as to not have one wander off which would almost certainly result in death. Sounds a lot like parenting, doesn't it? Parents, we know the way, we go the way, and then we show the way. We embrace the truth of God's word for ourselves, we model Christ's likeness before our children; then, we point their hearts toward a loving Savior after which we trust the Holy Spirit to work in their hearts.

LIVE IT

In 1 Corinthians, the Apostle Paul writes to the church at Corinth that they should follow his example as he follows the example of Christ. Other versions of the scripture say imitate. Can your children imitate your behavior? Would their imitation of you be spot on? Would it be reflective of a relationship rooted in Christ? If they did a parody of you on Saturday Night Live, would it glorify or grieve the Holy Spirit? Parents, live a life worth imitating. Do your children see you pray? Do your children see you serve? Do your children experience your fruit of the spirit?

The things which you learned and received and heard and saw in me, these do, and the God of peace will be with you. Philippians 4:9

GIVE IT

Ready your children for God's use by actively sharing your faith with them. It is God's desire that none should perish and He intends for the knowledge of who He is to be passed through the familial line. God is expecting us to raise a generation of believers. I do not want my children to adopt the faith simply because it's what I believe. I want them to adopt the faith because it is The Way, The Truth and The Life. Today's Millennials are abandoning the faith in droves. Nearly six in ten who grew up in church have walked away.[2] We don't want to raise a generation of half-hearted believers who only serve God in deed but whose hearts are far from Him. We give our faith to our children by the way we live, by declaring the praiseworthy deeds of the Lord, by maximizing teachable moments, and by helping them "see" God in every facet of daily living.

> *For I have known him, in order that he may command his children and his household after him, that they keep the way of the LORD, to do righteousness and justice, that the LORD may bring to Abraham what He has spoken to him. Genesis 18:19*

NURTURE IT

As we live out our faith, then actively share it with our children, we carefully tend their budding curiosity about God. We stoke the flames by continuing to be approachable. If they feel comfortable to talk to us about puberty, surely, they'll know they can come to us with their burning questions about God. We'd just better be prepared to have an answer. 1 Peter 3:15 tells us to be ready to have an answer for this hope we have. And to have an answer means that we must continually study God's word and hear His voice for fresh insight and obey what He tells us to do. How beautiful it will be to engage in a lively discussion with your children about how good your God really is.

God is very clear and His word is very direct. He has a plan and purpose for your child. His plans for your child are instrumental in His work of building the kingdom here on Earth. He has a specific role for you as the parent to shepherd your children, keeping watch over them until they come to know Him for themselves. In chapters 1 & 2, we've dug deep. We've examined where we are and what God has to say about children and about parenting. Now it's time to push our sleeves up and put our comfortable shoes on as we walk out the practical "how to's" of purposeful parenting. But before we do, let's do a practical application and then, let's pray.

PRACTICAL APPLICATION

Together with your children, create your family tree. Get creative and have fun with it. From a digital version to a tree made from a paper bag, the possibilities are endless. As you create the tree, talk about God's plans and purposes for the family and how God transfers blessings through the family line.

prayer

To the One whose plans and purposes are always sure and are always good, we bless your name. We marvel at how you operate. You are a God of order. You are a God of purpose. Nothing is happenstance with you. Oh Adonai, you are Lord of all. Lord forgive me for any time I placed my will and my plans above yours. I can attempt to plan my way but it is you that orders my steps. Help me remember that my children belong to you and not to me. Let me always celebrate the fearfully and wonderfully made persons you created them to be and not try to manipulate your perfect design for their lives. You made each of my children special. As a part of your divine plan, you sent these children to me. By the power of the Holy Spirit, I will rise up and be the parent you've called me to be.

⤝

Chapter 3

CONNECTING WITH THE HEART

Above all else, guard your heart, for everything
you do flows from it. Proverbs 4:23

SO MUCH OF PARENTAL LIFE is consumed with meeting temporal needs. Endless piles of laundry, shuttling children to and from activities, cooking meals, you know the drill. Not to mention adding in the amount of time, energy and effort expended in trying to get children to DO things they really could care less about or to get them to STOP doing things they are perfectly content with. Perhaps you're ready to blow a gasket because you've told your pre-teen boy for the millionth time that he needs to shower daily. And you can't recall how many times you've told your toddler not to jump on the furniture. While requests for showering and not jumping on furniture are reasonable, they do not serve as an investment in connecting with the hearts of our children.

The job of parenting may find us doing many seemingly important things for our children. But we want to be cautious to not miss out on the needed thing. Just as Jesus affirmed that Mary had chosen the better part, let us choose the better part and that is connecting with the hearts of our children. So how do we connect with our children when most of our daily interactions are moving them through to the next activity? Through purposeful, meaningful interaction, we will seize the opportunity to tend the garden of our children's hearts for everything they think, say and do flows from the heart space.

Nobel Peace Prize recipient and novelist, Toni Morrison appeared on an episode of Oprah's *Lifeclass*. On the show, the prolific author dispensed this wisdom:

> *"It's interesting to see when a kid walks into the room... does your face light up? That's what they're looking for... when my children used to walk in the room when they were little, I looked at them to see if they had buckled their trousers or if their hair was combed or their socks were up...so you think your affection and your deep love is on display 'cause you're caring for them; it's not. When they see you, they see the critical face...what's wrong now?... But, then if you let your face speak what's in your heart... Because when they walked in the room I was glad to see them. It's just as small as that, you see."[3]*

She so eloquently illustrated the difference between meeting temporal needs and maximizing on the opportunity to connect with the heart. Oprah went on to say that one of her biggest learning lessons of the early 90's was that the common denominator in the human experience is that everyone wants to be appreciated or validated. Given that, what are we teaching our children by spending so much energy on things that may not matter in five years, much less ten? How many moments will we have missed? How many hugs would not have been shared? How many smiles would have been deterred?

How will our children feel about themselves if the words we dispense are focused on what they haven't done right, what they aren't doing or what they have done wrong?

"You haven't…"

"You aren't…"

"When will you ever…"

"You can't…"

"You won't…"

"Don't…"

"Stop…"

"No…"

Yup, I've said them all too but I'm learning to do better. It requires reframing the dialogue. "Well, what CAN I do then?" That's what their hearts want to know. Purpose to fill their hearts with what they CAN do.

With your birth children, connecting with the heart begins in the womb. For 40 weeks, the child has heard mom's voice.

They've heard and felt mom's heartbeat. They know mom's smell. Immediately post delivery, if skin to skin contact is made, a flood of oxytocin, sometimes called the love hormone, is released connecting the hearts of mother and baby. From this point forward, life continues to present many opportunities to connect with the heart. Even if the child is not your flesh and blood, the opportunities still exist. Research Professor Dr. Brene Brown says, *"We are hardwired to connect with others, it's what gives purpose and meaning to our lives, and without it there is suffering."* Will you help minimize suffering by proactively connecting with the hearts of your children?

GENTLENESS

Capturing our children's hearts begins with a gentle approach. If you grew up with persons that were rough, harsh or rigid, gentleness may be foreign to you. Pray for a spirit of gentleness. What does gentleness look like? When you are gentle, your face softens. Your eyes relax. Your tone of voice is light and joyous. Even if you are giving a command, your voice is firm but devoid of harshness. You reach out in love. When you extend your hand toward your child, does he or she move toward you or recoil in the opposite direction?

Jesus himself models gentleness for us. Though He is ALL-powerful, He shows us His true power in being gentle. How easy would it have been for Him to be harsh to the Pharisee? When He was lied upon, misunderstood and even betrayed, He maintained a spirit of gentleness. His power at work in you enables you to be gentle too.

Take my yoke upon you and learn from me, for I am gentle and humble in heart, and you will find rest for your souls. Matthew 11:29

The wrath of man does not produce the righteousness of God. Spewing harsh words is like a torrent of hot vomit cascading over the child, much like the flow of lava from a volcano destroying everything in its wake. Then you're left with the aftereffect of ash hanging in the air for years, stifling growth. Harshness does not draw the heart closer. In fact, harshness creates a wedge in your relationships.

Let's face it; we do live in a harsh world. I used to think I needed to toughen my children up so they would have thick skin to survive in this cruel world. But I thank God for His example and for His gentle guidance. His redirection to truth said, "Be gentle with your children. This world doesn't need more harsh people but needs more kind, gentle, compassionate souls who will heal the world with love". Let us be quick to catch this one. I have a child that is gentle, sensitive, and compassionate. She's been teased for being sensitive. She's been called a crybaby and told she needs to get tougher skin. But I affirm this child because our world needs more tenderhearted souls like her.

HUMILITY

In order to join hearts with our children, we have to be humble. There's no way around it; parenting requires humility. I know you think you know a lot and yes you do. But parenting isn't about who knows more. You are not in a contest with your child over who knows more. Humility is realizing that, yes, you have limitations. Humility is coming face to face with the fact that you are nothing and can do nothing apart from Christ. He is the source of your strength and you certainly can't parent without Him.

Pride is the source of many of the problems that plague our world. Be reminded, pride comes before the fall. Yes, parent, you can fall and fail merely by thinking more highly of yourself than you ought. The proud parent can be a bully. The proud parent doesn't say, "I'm sorry." The humble parent recognizes they don't have all the answers. The humble parent knows they're learning day to day along with their children. True humility is the mark of one who is mature. "Humble myself to a child? You sound crazy!" Is that what you're thinking? Well, just try it and see.

Jesus himself is an excellent embodiment of humility. The bible says, *"rather, he made himself nothing by taking the very nature of a servant, being made in human likeness."* Philippians 2:7 Though He is all knowing, all-powerful and divine, He does not flaunt or abuse His position. His position of humility draws others into relationship with Him. And the same can be said of your role in parenting. Assuming a place of humility can draw your children into closer relationship with you. While it is true that you occupy the position of authority, it is useful to lay a common ground of mutual love and respect. And we find this common ground when we humble ourselves, surrender control and listen with the heart.

Well, let's clear this up right now. Children are not your property or your possession. You have just been given stewardship over them. When you are a steward, that means you are accountable for and responsible for. Your job then is to lead and guide, not to control or manipulate. Besides, you can't MAKE anyone do anything. In the early childhood years, you can wield a temporary sense of control but as they enter pre-teen years, you'll see that it was just that: false control. You do not own them. They are individual thinking, feeling, and acting beings.

CONNECTEDNESS

The thread that runs through effective communication is connectedness. We have to connect with the heart before we attempt to dispense information. We see Jesus do this time and again. He asks a question as a means of gently inviting His people into a dialogue with Him. We see Jesus ask the Samaritan woman for a drink. We see Jesus ask His disciples why they are afraid. He asks Peter, "Who do you say I am?" He even asks the Father why He's been forsaken.

A gateway to any resolution is caring. Your child must first know you care and caring is found in connectedness. If you haven't been making regular deposits emotionally, they are less likely to be receptive and may reject your advances. Connectedness occurs when you intentionally seek to engage in their world. Connectedness is about doing life together. Doing life together not just a popular hashtag for marriage but is a powerful illustration of engaging and connecting with your children.

VULNERABILITY

This issue arises again. It is really the key to unlocking the heart. Are you open enough to share your own hurts, feelings and disappointments with your children? Are you willing to share your failures? I encourage you to share your feelings with your child. And while you're sharing your feelings with your child, create space for them to share too. Parents typically tell their children what the child ought to feel. It's typical for a parent to negate, deny or simply ignore a child's feelings. Have you ever said,

"You're OK."

"It didn't hurt that much."

"You'll be alright."

"Don't worry about it."

How about we try a different approach and empathize with them instead? Recall what it felt like when you were hurt or disappointed and meet your child from that seat of emotion. When your child is hurt, acknowledge their hurt. Then go a step further and share a time you've been hurt.

Recently, my daughter got an 80% on a test. The test had to be signed by me, then returned to the teacher. As I was signing, I noticed big fat teardrops forming in my baby's eyes. She began to cry silently. This is the sensitive one I mentioned earlier. I asked her why she was crying. She said an 80 was a B and a B was not good. I went on to explain to her that a B was still a good grade, to which she replied it was not good enough. Can I be completely honest with y'all? At this point, I wanted to tell her, *"You'll be alright",* for her to put that paper in the bag and be done with it. I was thinking, *"Little girl, it's nothing. You'll be fine! Wait until you're an adult then you'll know what real problems feel like."* Please don't judge me but those were my thoughts at that moment. But then I remembered, what she needed in that moment was not only reassurance but also empathy. She needed a partner who knew what it felt like to come up short. So, I pointed out that she usually gets A's and affirmed that when we do less than our usual best, it can hurt. I shared with her a story about my cooking. My children think I'm a great chef—their words not mine. But every now and again, I have an EPIC cooking fail. And one occurred when I was baking for a ministry event. I had talked about this pumpkin bread. Yes, I would deliver THE BEST pumpkin bread to this fellowship. Well, the bread never cooked in the middle, even after having been in the oven for an hour and a half. My daughter smiled sweetly and chuckled a bit as her mood lightened. About 10 minutes later, she came and handed me a white board upon which she had written, *"I love that mommy loves me and helps me be happy when I am sad".* She even added some flair by drawing her favorite tongue sticking out, winking emoji. Yup; she needed me to expose myself, to share in her hurt, to be vulnerable.

Gentleness, humility, connectedness and vulnerability lay the framework for effective communication. When we adults have disarmed ourselves and become accessible to our children, they are more apt to open up and heart connections can be forged. This truth is vital to embrace as it paves the way for open and honest dialogue. God wants you to be tenderhearted so that you can connect hearts with your children.

> *And I will give you a new heart, and a new spirit I will put within you. And I will remove the heart of stone from your flesh and give you a heart of flesh. Ezekiel 36:26*

We want our children to feel comfortable enough to share anything with us. We want to be their "go to" source for information. We want to be their sounding board for things that are confusing or frustrating. And the road is made passable when we show that we are approachable by being gentle, humble, connected and vulnerable. When you have done this, your own heart has been primed for connection. The next step is to extend yourself to your child through open communication.

OPEN COMMUNICATION

When you listen empathetically and connect emotionally, the atmosphere is ripe for open communication. There are times when we can miss the mark in communicating with our children because we both have our vantage points of truth. There are times when those truths can seem like polar opposites. Let me give you an illustration.

It was a trip that promised to be filled with fun, food, and laughs-a-plenty. Four girlfriends headed to The Big Easy—New Orleans—for an annual music festival that draws nearly half a million participants. Now who can go to New Orleans and not want to experience real Creole and Cajun food? No trip would be complete without beignets at Café Du Monde, gumbo at Dooky Chase and a po-boy at Domilise's.

Well, the locals said you've got to visit Two Sisters. So, the friends set about their day. Two deciding to venture off together, one deciding to sleep late and one to catch a book signing after which they'd all meet for lunch. Well, three of the friends did, indeed, meet up at Two Sisters and were seated at an elegant table, while one friend stood in a long line at Two Sisters.

Feet swelling in the sweltering New Orleans July heat, the straps on my sandals dug into my fleshy dogs. My cell phone had died so I couldn't call my sisters to see what was taking them so long. After waiting for over an hour, I decided to cut my losses, order food and go back to the hotel. Wouldn't you know it; they were out of EVERYTHING I could eat. Needless to say, I was hot, hungry and heated! When I reconnected with my sisters to find out why they never showed up, it was then that we realized that there were TWO restaurants in New Orleans called Two Sisters. We were both operating in separate truths.

I would caution you to not become hot and heated as I did on that steamy July day. Instead, communicate with your child with an open heart and a listening ear. When we focus solely on one set of details, we can miss another causing a breakdown in communication, which can lead to conflict. Your child may have a valid but different truth and connecting with the heart enables you to hear their truth.

Let me share with you another illustration from the 12 year-old perspective. Driving on the way to her birthday dinner, I overheard my daughter and her friend exchanging tales about their parents. There was resounding mutual agreement about chores, discipline and never-ending learning. Then my daughter proceeded to talk about me and it went a little like this, "She's the one that told me to scrub the pots on the counter. When I scrubbed the pots on the counter, I got in trouble."

Did you all catch that? Indeed, I told her to scrub the pots on the counter. When I said that, I meant that she was to take the pots that were sitting on the counter and place them into the sink and scrub them there. Her brain understood, scrub the pots while they were still sitting on top of the counter. One message understood two ways. Parents, when you send a message, you have to be sure the message is heard, clarified, then responded to. Otherwise, the cycle of communication is broken. Can you see how some of the misunderstandings you have with your children may just be because you interpret things differently?

THE INVITATION

How do you invite your children's gaze and attention? They beckon for your gaze. They long for your attention. In Chapter 6, we'll talk more about their cry to be seen. But for now, let's address how you extend yourself to open the lines of communication with your children. Are they integral parts of your day or merely spectators to your busy doing? Do you seek to actively engage them in conversation, or do you wait for them to talk to you? Do you approach them only when there is a problem to be addressed? Receiving an invitation is a welcomed occurrence. The guest of honor feels blessed and honored to have you show up. The same can be said for inviting your children. They are blessed and feel honored when you invite their gaze and attention.

LISTENING WITH THE HEART

Think about the dialogue you've exchanged with your child in the last 24 hours. Really. Pause and think about it. Was most of it affirming or corrective in nature? We tend to do more talking about what we see that needs to be fixed. I've heard it said you have one mouth and two ears for a reason and that's to do twice as much listening. While parenting does require us to download a great deal of information primarily through talking, I would suggest we do more listening.

And when your children are talking, how do you show that you are listening? Are you staring at the screen of your phone? Are you talking to them while in separate rooms? When they are attempting to engage you in dialogue, are you giving clipped answers like huh, mm-hmm, and mmm yeah? Tally up the minutes you've spent watching TV, social media, on the phone and the like. Does it equate with the amount of uninterrupted, focused attention given to your child? When you tell your child, *"Just a minute,"* do you get back to them within a minute? Open communication demands that you listen with the heart.

When you listen with an open heart, you hear them out. You give full, focused attention, including eye contact. Don't be in such a hurry to find a solution for what they're sharing (women, you know we despise when men do this to us when we are simply looking for an empathetic ear). Intentionally tell yourself, "I'm connecting with the heart so I'll be slow to speak." Ask yourself, "What are they really trying to tell to me?" Even when you don't agree, give your child room to talk. Affirm their courage to share with you by saying, "I appreciate you telling me." Restate to ensure understanding by starting with, "What I hear you saying is...".

When you listen, are you multitasking? Are you formulating responses in your mind while they're talking? Are you distracted with your personal thoughts? Are you engaged in another activity? Occasionally, I have to remind my children to please ensure they have my full attention before trying to tell me something. I want to do my best to connect with them. Sometimes they'll begin talking when I'm engaged with another child. I'd like to avoid someone telling me on the drive to school in the morning, "Mommy, I reminded you about the field trip money last night". "When was that?" I ask? "When you were in the laundry room" they say. Yup; I heard nothing with my head half way in the dryer. Parents, you make it your business to be heard, right? Some parents go to great lengths to get their points across: yelling, lecturing, and repeating the same things over and over. Let us be just as tenacious in hearing as we are with being heard.

When we listen, we aren't only listening to what they say; we are also receiving information from their non-verbal cues. In fact, most of our communication is done without speaking. Communication is comprised of 7% words we say, 38% tone & inflection and 55% body language.[4] Our children are consistently communicating information, thoughts and emotions. The key is for us to be open, receptive, and gently responsive as they attempt to connect.

REMOVE THE BARRIERS

Given that communication is loaded with so much spoken and unstated information, there are bound to be some roadblocks. The whole approach of connecting with the heart attempts to ward off breakdowns in communication. Being gentle, humble, connected and vulnerable lay fresh pavement for effective communication. Then being open, inviting them and listening with the heart gives them the green light to GO forward in sharing with you. Just like we can get stuck in traffic on the way to a job interview, our communication with our children can bottleneck. We can even experience gridlock, with communication coming to a complete standstill.

Let's examine some common communication barriers. What debris have children thrown onto Communication Avenue? They may talk back or argue. You ever have a child give you the silent treatment? On first glance, it may seem they are quiet or obedient but upon investigation, you see them stewing beneath that quiet veneer. That can be a manipulation tactic or a passive-aggressive power play. Perhaps your child pitches attitude, huffing of breath, slumping shoulders, sucking teeth, dragging feet, you get the picture.

But wait a minute, you've got some road kill on Communication Avenue too. Instead of asking a question, you proceed with a rapid-fire interrogation, like a courtroom prosecutor. Do you interrupt when they are speaking? Do you jump to conclusions and finish the story for them before they've had a chance to explain? Are you physically present but emotionally unavailable because you've got too much on the mind? Are you unapproachable? Do you make accusations before fully gathering all necessary information? Do you react versus respond? Are you always chomping at the bit to give advice instead of leading them to self-discovery? Do you dispense too much information when it's not necessary? Do you lose your temper? Are you impatient? Do you tell them how they're feeling when they're trying to tell you the opposite? It looks like we are the ones causing the traffic jam. It's no wonder they shut down.

The road can become even more treacherous when we factor in ages and stages of development. Developmentally, children may not have acquired the skills to pivot and turn away from communication litter in the road. Poor children; they really are doing the best they can with the communication skills they've acquired in their few short years of living. And when they've tried to communicate, we may have created an environment non-conducive to communication. Remember parents, based on age, some of their actions and reactions are hormonal and difficult for them to navigate. While you have (say your age) years of life experience to draw upon when making a decision, they aren't where you are. So, parents, the onus is on us to keep the communication highway free and clear of debris and to keep the pavement nice and smooth as potholes are bound to appear after a storm. More listening and less talking.

Too often we underestimate the power of a touch, a smile, a kind word, a listening ear, an honest compliment, or the smallest act of caring, all of which have the potential to turn a life around. Leo Buscaglia

KNOW THEM

We can further reach toward our children to connect hearts by knowing them. Do you really know each of your children on a personal level? What makes them most joyful? What makes them sad? How do they see themselves within the context of the family? Do you know who they eat lunch with at school? Do you know their deepest fears? You gain this information by becoming a student. You are the student and your child is your subject of learning.

Jones, in the book *The Noticer* by Andy Andrews, had a special gift. He had a way of seeing; a gift of noticing things others missed. Be like Jones having eyes to see what others miss. How do you get this kind of sight? One way mentioned earlier is by listening with the heart. Out of the abundance of the heart, the mouth speaks so your children will tell you what's in their hearts. You've just got to be attentively listening. Keen observation leads to great insight. Observe how they navigate a roomful of strangers. How do they move about the playground? For those with more than one child in the home, spend time with each, one on one. Yes, it can be done. I've got six children and while I long to see 9pm so I can "shut down", I've usually got a little person snuggled up with me for one on one time.

Another strategy I've adopted comes from a wonderful, loving mother of eight. She introduced me to the idea of keeping a "mommy & me" journal. The journals can be used to share whatever is on the heart. Entries don't have to be long and exhaustive. But it lays more pavement for clear roads of communication and allows us to learn more about them. It is just another way to connect hearts and get to know them. Recently, I saw a "mommy and me" journal that came with writing prompts in it. Another suggestion is to have one-on-one outings as a way to get to know more about your child.

Knowing your children proactively sets you up for more heart connections. By getting to know them, I've learned one of my children connects and feels loved through physical touch. By nature, I am a touchy feely person. I love to give cuddles and hugs. But after nursing a baby every two hours (being touched), having the fat on my back rubbed by my touchy toddler (touched some more), when my son whose love language is TOUCH comes along, I'm all touched out! No more touching mommy please and thank you! But knowing my child's need, each day when he is dismissed from school and comes sauntering toward the car, I step out and give him a rub on the head. It is a simple, gentle reassurance that affirms I know you, I see you and I love you.

PURPOSEFUL ENCOURAGEMENT

Since so much of our dialogue with children is corrective in nature, it is critical that we are intentional about giving words of affirmation. If we attempt to correct them when no deposit has been made, we'll end up overdrawing their emotional accounts. Put on your empathy hat and imagine every verbal interaction with your boss being corrective in nature. Imagine, if every time you talked to them, they negated, denied, ignored or corrected what you've just said. Over time, how would you view your boss? When you saw him approaching how would you feel? Don't be that boss. Instead, you are the boss everyone raves about. You have high expectations but everyone loves working for you because you are supportive and encouraging.

I say it so often my kids can recite it by heart. *"Do not let any unwholesome talk come out of your mouths, but only what is helpful for building others up according to their needs, that it may benefit those who listen." Ephesians 4:29.* I say it over and over. When my children say something unkind to a sibling, I gently chide, "Was that wholesome talk?" "Is that building your sister up?" One day, one of my children was being especially slothful during homework time. "Quick lips" mommy set about getting that child straight. "Working at this pace will *never* cut it in high school. It's not like middle school you know. You'd better get it together and get it together QUICK!" Then came the gentle tap on the shoulder as the Holy Spirit whispered, "Is that wholesome talk, building her up?" Can you say 'convicted?' Yes! This mama has got to practice what she preaches.

God's tap on the shoulder caused me to do some self-examination. Why was "loose lips" mommy so quick to react to this child moving slowly through her homework? It boiled down to fear. In a matter of seconds, I envision this child, who is normally an excellent student, floundering in high school. In my mind, I saw this child who used to be a big fish in a little pond, now a little fish in a big pond being gobbled up by brighter, fast fish. FEAR. The voice of the critical parent is the voice of fear. Dig in and uproot that fear so you can move forward in purposeful encouragement.

What does purposeful encouragement sound like? Your child hears from you what they've done and the impact it had. "Wow, I'm impressed with the progress you are making in playing the recorder. I was so proud when I saw you look up a video for the song you were struggling with. That's determination and your efforts are paying off. You nailed the song!" (This was an actual conversation I had with my son). On a side note, this child went on to continue practicing after bedtime. I must admit I cherish bedtime. Because I have so much "face" time with my children from 6:00am-9:00pm, I relish the few minutes of quiet at night. Sure enough, here he was playing the recorder. But you know what? I let him play. I put my own desire for quiet aside. Just a short time earlier, I affirmed him for his efforts. He was really trying his best and just wanted more time for practice. Parents, are you willing to be inconvenienced for the greater good?

Our purposeful encouragement serves to build them up. Jeremiah 24:6 says, *For I will set My eyes on them for good, and I will bring them back to this land; I will build them and not pull them down, and I will plant them and not pluck them up.* Parents, our words have the ability to pluck them up. Let's not undo our own efforts at planting. God has provided good seed. Our children are good seed. We've already laid rich fertile soil. The Son and His rivers of living are bringing about increase. We will fertilize the plant through words of affirmation. We will speak life. We will speak blessing. We will speak well of them to them. We will be purposeful encouragers.

....

PRACTICAL APPLICATION

Start a "mom and me" journal. The journal can be any type of notebook. The journal gives you and your child a place to connect with the heart. Each day or once a week, check in by writing your child a question, observing something that happened, something you want to acknowledge or something you want to clarify. Then give the notebook to your child and have them write back. If you're the artsy type, you can even decorate the cover. Have fun with it.

....

prayer

Eternal One and lover of my soul, thank you for always extending yourself and seeking to connect with my heart. I pray that you will open the eyes of my heart so that I will be available to my children. Enable me to connect with their hearts through purposeful interactions. May I present myself gentle, humble and vulnerable so that they feel I am approachable. May I keep my eyes and ears open so that I can learn who they are and know them deeply. May my words be filled with grace. May I be intentional in maximizing opportunities to communicate with them. Knit me closer to my children now and evermore.

⤖

$Chapter\ 4$

LOVE AND ACCEPTANCE

"Love is patient, love is kind. It does not envy, it does not boast, it is not proud. It does not dishonor others, it is not self-seeking, it is not easily angered, it keeps no record of wrongs. Love does not delight in evil but rejoices with the truth. It always protects, always trusts, always hopes, always perseveres. Love never fails. But where there are prophecies, they will cease; where there are tongues, they will be stilled; where there is knowledge, it will pass away." 1 Corinthians 13:4-8

I WANT TO INVITE YOU in. Come real close. Ever closer. I want to give you a glimpse into my heart. I'd love for you to see a heart that beats in time, in perfect concert with the Father. But when I remove the rose-colored filter from the doorway of my heart, you'll see a heart that's prone to sin. When my daughter immediately obeys, oh, how my heart soars. I can pat her shoulder, be chatty with her, and make direct eye contact, all demonstrations of genuine love. But if she doesn't obey, depending on my current spiritual and emotional state…well, let's just say conditional love is what I dish out.

Have you ever intentionally withheld eye contact as a means of punishing a child because they said or did something you did not like? Have you ever refused to physically embrace a child because you were upset with their behavior? That, my friend is conditional love; I'll show you I love you when you behave the way I want you to behave.

Let's examine then a portrait of true love. The heading of this chapter in my bible is called *The Greatest Gift*. You can find the verses on the preceding page. Read it slowly and let its truth pierce your heart. Yes; turn the page back and read it. SLOWLY. Now, let's walk through these verses.

LOVE IS PATIENT

Have you ever prayed for patience? I think it's one of those things that we ask for, not understanding what we are really asking for. The fact of the matter is, in order to be a patient person, your patience has to be developed; it has to be stretched, worked and tested. While there are some that are inherently patient, for most it is a trait that is cultivated. The word "patience" sounds pretty, even lyrical. Go ahead, say it. Let it flow off your lips; *PATIENCE*. It sounds lovely but when lived out more closely resembles long-suffering, forbearance, endurance, restraint and tolerance. Do those synonyms paint a different picture in your mind?

The patient parent calmly finds solutions to help her son with his math homework when he's really struggling and you are both overly frustrated. The patient parent plays "doll dress up" for over an hour when you really want to finish cleaning the kitchen. The patient parent creates extra time in the morning routine for his son to ride his skateboard for 5 minutes before leaving for school in the morning, knowing that activity helps him release physical energy before having to sit down in a classroom for hours. Your patient interactions with your children let them know you value them.

LOVE IS KIND

Go back to your 4th grade classroom. Think of the child in your class who was kind. She immediately pops into my head. My kind classmate was Sandy Cheung. She always had a gentle response and her eyes softened when she spoke. And why can I remember that all these years later? Because kindness leaves a lasting impression, as does harshness. We would fare better sowing seeds of kindness into the fertile soil of our children's hearts. Kindness has a way of deescalating even the most intense situations.

LOVE DOES NOT ENVY

Loving parents teach their child contentment. Envy is stealthy and can easily creep into our children's hearts. Our children can begin to crave things others have. While it's typical for children to want things, the burden of responsibility lies on the parent to know when to say no and when to indulge. Have you ever purchased things for your child out of guilt or not wanting your child to feel left out? Have you given a young child an elaborate gift or party? Was the motivation for that really for the child's enjoyment or to fill some other need? Have you felt pressured to supply your children with the latest electronics or clothing? Examine the root cause for why you give your children some of the things they have. Let's be intentional to cultivate hearts that are content. And if you see your children being envious of what others have, be sure to address it directly, exploring why they want the thing and affirming what God has for them is for them.

LOVE DOES NOT BOAST

"I'm the parent here!" Have you ever said that one? Does the obvious warrant stating? And what exactly are you trying to communicate when you say that? Do we see Jesus telling the disciples, "Look, I'm the King of Kings and Lord of Lords up in here and you will do as I say!"? Nope; we don't see that. What we see Jesus saying is:

- I've come to serve (Matthew 20:28)
- I do the will of Him who sent me (John 6:38)
- I merely say what the Father tells me to say (John 12:49).

We do not see Jesus boastful even when dealing with the Pharisee and Sadducee. So, let's take a note from Jesus and eliminate boasting. You're right. You are the parent. No need to throw the title around. You know those people who feel like they must say their title every time they talk to you? It gets on your nerves, right? Okay then. Don't be that person.

LOVE IS NOT PROUD

Parents tend to think more highly of themselves than they ought. The scriptures say a little yeast leavens the whole batch of dough. A little pride deems you prideful so remove the leaven. Scripture also talks about not being puffed up. Parents, when you feel yourself beginning to swell, use a word of kindness and see if it helps you remove the pride.

Pride shows up in parenting in many ways. You can be too proud to say, "I'm sorry" to your child. Your pride can trick you into believing you have all the right answers; thus, your child knows nothing so they should shut up and listen. Your pride can cause you to be self-absorbed. Pride can make you believe your parenting is superior to those parents around you. Pride can have you wrapped up in your children's achievements, taking the credit for yourself. Where there is complete love, there is no room for pride.

LOVE DOES NOT DISHONOR

To show honor is to esteem others higher than one's self. It is to show how special others are and to go out of our way in doing so. The opposite then, dishonor, strips our children of their value. Dishonor teaches them to "stay in a child's place." Be reminded that Jesus said, "the kingdom of heaven belongs to [them]." He also said, "unless we are like little children, we would not enter the kingdom." So, it would behoove us to recognize that even though they are younger than we are chronologically, they still hold a place of prominence in the kingdom and they deserve our honor. How do you plan to show honor to your children?

LOVE IS NOT SELF-SEEKING

You want what you want when you want it. You want them to be quiet because you're irritable. You want them to get honor roll so you can post the pictures on social media. You want to live vicariously through them because you feel like you missed out on something as a child or are trying to relive your glory days. You want what you want for them more than what God has destined for them. You attempt to carefully craft every facet of their lives. You try to forge and force what their personalities ought to be. You, you, you. Well that is a no, no, no. This is not about you. True love is not self-seeking but surrenders its own desire to receive the Lord's will His way.

LOVE IS NOT EASILY ANGERED

Are you easily angered? Do you find yourself erupting like Mount Vesuvius? Inherently, anger is not bad. It is how we act when under the influence of anger that poses a problem. Angry outbursts are an indication that there is something else going on within.

Before I became a parent, I could never have imagined being angry with a sweet little person; staring into the face of the child you carried in the womb, a delicate tender little human. Nope; I could never. Then came days filled with sleepless nights, too much work, financial strain, and before you knew it, laid back *Bruce Banner* has given way to the raging *Hulk*.

Love demands you move beyond yourself and allow the fruit of the spirit to minister. God has given you a spirit of self-control. He has given you a spirit of gentleness. Let the joy of the Lord be your strength. Do not use anger to answer anger, as it will only escalate the situation. Respond in love to diffuse the situation and get to the heart of the underlying issue. Remember that the wrath of man does not produce the righteousness of God (James 1:20).

He's my lion and lamb child. Gentle, loving and affectionate but also obstinate, strong-willed and sometimes angry. He believes in justice and will fight for it. He's a protector and a defender. Occasionally, when given an instruction that requires him to break away from what he's currently doing, he gets angry or cries. When I attempt to deescalate the situation and diffuse his anger, sometimes he huffs his breath, flairs his nostrils or tightens his face in a grimacing scowl.

One day as I looked into that sweet face that was filled with anger, instead of seeing a hostile child that was ready to explode, I saw my loving little boy and it made me smile. Wait! Did he just smile back at me? Get this; we were in the middle of an intense moment and it was diffused with just one smile. Well, the next time he got angry, I tried it again. He was bound up in the angry face. I looked him directly in the eye and smiled. He mirrored my smile but then quickly tried to force his angry face back on. But it was too late. I had seen that cheery, missing tooth grin. I told him, "Yup, I already saw it. You already showed me your smiley face." We then engaged in a conversation about what caused him to be upset. The old pattern of escalating anger had been doused with a simple smile.

LOVE KEEPS NO RECORD OF WRONG

Have you ever gotten into an argument with someone you are in a relationship with and the person proceeded to list the litany of things you've ever done? Can you place yourself right in the seat of that emotion? I would guess that didn't feel good at all. So, imagine doing that to your child. When we use words like, "Every time", "How many times", "Didn't I tell you last time", we are keeping a record of wrong. Bear in mind, love covers a multitude of sins (1 Peter 4:8). And your Father in heaven casts your sins into the depths of the sea, remembering them no more. Will you take His lead and do the same for your children?

And while we're at it, we don't give children enough credit. We are quick to recount their wrongs but slow to recognize their good works. So, they may occasionally tell a tall tale, or even outright lie. But why do we generally doubt what they say? I've even been flat out guilty of telling a child they were wrong about something when, in fact, they were correct. Children are brilliant. They have great ideas. Listen to them. Take them up on their ideas and suggestions.

One time, my husband and I were caught outside in a torrential rainstorm. My husband was standing under an awning trying to think of the best possible way to make it to the car without getting completely soaked. My ten-year old who has the ability to "see" a situation and assess it quickly suggested that we drive to the upper level of this concourse as the upper level had an awning while the lower level we were on had no covering. And wouldn't you know, he was right. My husband followed his suggested path and managed to stay dry. Recently, I was listening to the son of a friend explain to his father how to get to the child's soccer game. This game was happening at a field near my home so I knew where it was. This family lived 25 miles from there. The son was telling the father exactly which exit to take. The father questioned, expressing his doubt. I had to interject and confirm that the son was indeed correct. Let's affirm them. They've got good ideas. Parents, we know a lot but so do they.

LOVE DOES NOT DELIGHT IN EVIL

Let's just face it; sometimes sin feels good in the moment. It can feel good to discharge anger. It can feel good to overeat. But that feeling is generally temporary. We should not get comfortable in our sin nor allow our children to do so. Love does not get pleasure out of evil and does not delight in sinful behavior.

Our children will be blessed when they walk NOT in the counsel of the wicked, nor stand in the way of sinners, nor sit in the seat of scoffers. We want our children to take delight in the things of the Lord. Are we presenting them with the beauty of the gospel or feeding their delight for the things of the world? We'll be talking more about this in Chapter 8. Suffice it to say, God is love and He does not delight in evil.

LOVE REJOICES IN TRUTH

From a young age, children are prone to lie. You don't have to teach a child how to lie. They just seem to know how to do it, right? When one of my sons was three years old, he had a bathroom accident on the rug. Instead of telling me, he just hid the rug. When I asked if he'd seen the rug, he told me no with a straight face. He was trying to cover up. Considering we've been covering up since the days of Adam, it comes as no surprise. Thus, we have to be diligent in teaching our children to rejoice in truth. Today's postmodern culture asserts that there is no absolute truth and that truth is whatever we each deem it to be. What a tragedy. Parents, let us share with our children that emphatically there is right and wrong, that there is good and evil, and that there is truth and lies. Affirm for them that Jesus is the way, the truth and the life. When they lie, take your time to explain that the truth sets them free. That begins by letting them see us embrace truth. When someone calls or comes to the door, do you instruct them to lie and say you aren't there? If your child carries something out of the Dollar Store that wasn't paid for, do you go back and pay and explain to your child why that was necessary? Or do you just shrug your shoulders thinking, well, it was only a dollar? Lead by example in living out truth before your children.

LOVE PROTECTS

We've been called to protect. It is our responsibility to guard and duly filter what our children see and hear. If we're not careful, we can find ourselves at either end of the protection spectrum. On one end, to have no protection, parents give children too many liberties and too much freedom. On the other end, we have helicopter parents controlling every aspect of their children's lives. Either extreme positions them for a fall. When we are too liberal, they see and hear what their brains and bodies cannot properly process. When we shield them from every possible eventuality, they are ill equipped when they leave home and rest assured, one day they will leave home and when that time comes we want them to know how to choose well. They won't be able to do that if we've never given them the ability to choose.

LOVE TRUSTS

When you trust, you believe in. Love hopes for the best and believes the best about people. "Do you believe me?" That's what our children want to know. "Do you believe *in* me?" That's what their hearts yearn for. If they've lied to you, it may make you prone to not believe them in the future. What does that communicate to your children? It tells them they are liars. They can't be trusted. There is no true forgiveness.

My son once lied to me about eating a special slice of cake my husband had bought for me. Now, anytime something comes up missing from the fridge (which happens frequently in a house with eight people), I automatically assume it's him. I've accused him while he's maintained innocence. It was only after I found empty candy wrappers in another child's closet, that I realized the error of my ways. I had presumed him guilty for every missing or eaten food item since he had done it that one time. Was that fair? I had to apologize to my son. Love believes the best. Have you ever known a teacher to say all students start with an A? Give your child an A. Believe the best about them.

LOVE HOPES

What are we if we don't have hope? That is one of the primary devices of the enemy. He seeks to steal, kill and destroy our hope. He does this by telling us lies and planting seeds of doubt. He's so cunning, you may come to accept some of his lies as truth. He whispers, "You are failing in your job as a parent", "You'll never get it right", or "You know you're messing them up real bad". Do not buy that worthless bill of goods. Your hope is in Christ Jesus and THAT hope never fails. You are not failing as a parent. You are not the only parent going through something with your child. You are doing plenty of good for your children. In fact, God is causing everything to work together for your good and for the good of your child. God said He makes all things new and that's a promise you can place your hope in.

LOVE PERSEVERES

It takes grit and determination to persevere. On the rough parenting days, you must be firmly planted so that you don't give up. On the days when you wonder if they're listening, if they're getting it, if they'll succeed, if they'll be safe from harm, you've got to remind yourself to move beyond doubt, to remain hopeful and to persevere.

There's no way around it; when you're a parent you're in it for the long haul. Our culture has tried to reduce parenting to a short window of birth to eighteen. When true relationship and connectivity exist with your child, you aren't bound by socially accepted expiration dates. Your enduring love for your child will see you through newborn sleepless nights, toddler tantrums, identity crises, puberty, leaving the nest, and boomerang adult children who return home. Graceful perseverance requires you to have an eternal mindset. The future and hope God has destined for your child will come to fruition. Keeping your focus not on the minutia of the day but, instead, on the big picture may save you some gray hairs.

LOVE NEVER FAILS

Children are happy one minute, sad the next. Your child invites you to sit on her bed and chat one day, the next day she barely speaks. A friend has wounded them. They're struggling in school. They've got an illness. Sometimes you feel adept at helping them; sometimes you're at a loss. No matter the situation, love never fails. Love always wins. In his song, *Real Love*, Speech of Arrested Development sums it up quite perfectly.

> *"Of all the hard times I've endured, ain't nothing that real love can't cure. Of all the hard times that I feel, ain't nothing that real love can't heal."*

Exactly! Love conquers ALL. Love heals all. Love never fails. When all the talking and all the knowing has fallen away, love is all that will remain. So how about we wage war, a love war. Let's join arms and charge forward with #ALoveRevolution. When interacting with our children, no matter the situation or circumstance, remember; love never fails. Delivering love to them in a way they can perceive will never fail.

LOVE IS A VERB

So how do we show our love? Remember, love is a verb and is evidenced not only in what we say but also in what we do; and not only in what we do but doing so in a way that the person can receive. You may buy a child a trinket every time you go out of town for work yet, that child feels unloved. In your mind, you've been thinking about the child and looking forward to seeing the child. You know that you love this child. The child, on the other hand, receives the trinket, puts it to the side and proceeds to ask you many questions, at which point you are distracted as you sort through the pile of mail that's built up while you were away. The child is now sullen and quiet and you cannot understand why the child isn't happy and doesn't like the gift. What happened? Love speaks more than one language so parent and child have to be speaking the same language.

In his book, *How to Really Love Your Child*, Dr. D. Ross Campbell shares three primary ways children receive love. He says children know they are loved when they receive appropriate physical touch, direct eye contact and meaningful focused attention.[5] While one of the three he mentions may be predominant, children benefit from receiving all of them. Additionally, when showing love to children, it is important to be in close physical proximity. While this is not always possible, try as you may to get close to your child. Gently lift a chin when you are speaking to a child, put your hand on their shoulder, and make direct eye contact. These are all ways of expressing love. It shows the child, "you are important and all of my attention is on you in this moment."

When I lived in my former home, I felt like I always had the children right underfoot. It was easy to communicate with them as they were always in close proximity. When I moved into my current home, something changed. I found that I was raising my voice to get the children's attention. I was talking between rooms and hollering up the steps. One day, God opened my eyes to see and hear our communication. I just had to stand there and shake my head. Here I was talking to a child from another room. So much MORE communication is passed when people speak face to face and I was missing out on the fullness of our communication. The house was more spacious, indeed, but it crippled my former communication style. So, I had to be diligent in reclaiming our communication. Though it is more work, I make a conscious effort to get in close proximity when communicating. In this way, I am able to share my love through eye contact, physical touch and focused attention.

LOVE SEES

Love cries out to be acknowledged, seen, and validated. When a pregnant Hagar attempted to flee because of Sarai's cruelty, she was broken. But she had an encounter with el-Roi, the God Who Sees. Not only did the angel of the Lord see her there, he blessed her. Just as God saw Hagar sitting there, He sees you and He sees your children. That's what love does; love sees.

Our children, in their own unique way, cry out, "Do you see me?" Their behavior, good, bad or otherwise calls out, "I am here. Please see me." I've got one child who makes screeching, high pitched screaming noises. Repeatedly, I've asked him to stop this, explaining that it hurts my sensitive eardrums. One day when he did the shriek, I "saw" him. God played the scene for me in slow motion. I was engaged in a conversation with another of my children when the shriek came. I quickly turned and saw the two little eyes darting glances at me. The eyes were crying out, "Look at me. SEE ME!" So, this time, instead of saying my usual line of, "Please stop! You're hurting my ears!", I turned fully in his direction, rubbed him on the head and gave him a hug. All he wanted was to be seen.

Our hearts yearn for love. We are wired with a need for love. From studies of neonatal intensive care unit babies to those in orphanages, those who receive loving touch and conversation thrive as compared to those who do not. And as believers, we've been called to love, to love God and love one another.

> *"Teacher, which is the great commandment in the law?" Jesus said to him, " 'You shall love the Lord your God with all your heart, with all your soul, and with all your mind. This is the first and great commandment. And the second is like it: You shall love your neighbor as yourself.' On these two commandments hang all the Law and the Prophets." Matthew 22:36-4*

Love chooses to love. It is a purposeful decision and not just a feeling. Just as you choose to be cranky, or choose to put on a smile, love is a choice. In the William Barclay Daily Study Bible, of agape love it says, *"...Christian love is not an emotional thing. This agape is a thing, not only of the emotions, but also of the will. It is the ability to retain unconquerable good will to the unlovely and the unlovable, towards those who do not love us, and even towards those whom we do not like. Agape is that quality of mind and heart which compels a Christian never to feel any bitterness, never to feel any desire for revenge, but always to seek the highest good of every man no matter what he may be."*[6]

Loves chooses to love even when it hurts. Love chooses to love even when it's inconvenient. Love chooses people over projects. Purpose in your heart and mind to choose love. *"There is a terrible hunger for love. We all experience that in our lives—the pain, the loneliness. We must have the courage to recognize it. The poor you may have right in your own family. Find them. Love them."* Mother Teresa

LOVE IS UNBIASED

You know the saying, "I love all my children equally." But is that really possible? If you only have one child, then I guess that's true. But anyone with more than one child knows you love them *differently*. It's not about equanimity but about individuality. To think that you can love them equally is a fallacy. Each child is fearfully and wonderfully made to be different, thus, requiring you to love them differently. And let's face it, some are just easier to love than others. We'll address this more in a bit when we talk about acceptance. My 'tween recently read a study that reported attractive children in the family are disciplined less. I can attest that many factors do, in fact, influence my ability to love my children. Hence, the need for God to work in and through me in my parenting.

Loving them calls for us to adapt our approach based on temperament, maturity, and many other factors. Equal love is not the goal but loving based on the individual needs of the child. If you've got more than one child, inevitably, they will perceive and receive love differently. When they're adults, they'll probably exchange notes on whom mom or dad loved more. It's all very subjective. Just purpose to connect hearts individually as that is the key to unbiased love.

LOVE FORGIVES

"Mommy, so you love me even when I don't wisten?" asked my sweet three-year old. He had disobeyed me. After talking to him about his actions, all he wanted was affirmation that we were still good. His tender heart wanted reassurance that even when he does something I don't approve of that he will still be loved, be accepted and be forgiven.

Parents, oh, how easy it is to fall into the snare of unforgiveness. We can take it quite personally when a child sins. We can feel as if they've done it to intentionally spite us. And because of that, we can harbor unforgiveness. Unforgiveness plants a root of resentfulness. That root of resentfulness grows into a tree of bitterness and that tree of bitterness spawns fruit of anger and the seeds within the fruit of anger can lead to rage. Can you see the cycle of toxicity that unforgiveness can bring? That deadly cycle can be thwarted with forgiveness.

Your child deserves to be forgiven. Just as Christ forgives you day by day for your offenses, you ought to extend that same forgiveness. Your child needs to be affirmed. They need to know that when they sin they are still loved. Through prayer, we attack the sin, not the child. In Mark 11, Jesus admonishes us to forgive.

He says whenever we stand praying, to forgive. Imagine that; for every time you set yourself to pray, you are reminded to forgive. I would venture to say Jesus knows the dark, deep root that unforgiveness can sow, thus, He instructs us to continually come before the altar laying it down. Reassure your child; yes; even when you don't "wisten", I still love you. You are forgiven.

> *"People need loving the most when they deserve it the least." Louise Hay*

ACCEPTANCE

It is not inherently easy to accept those different than us. It can be even harder when those persons are your own children. You can be plagued with guilt for not accepting your child. After all, this child is a part of you. Rejecting some part of your child is like rejecting a part of yourself. That can do something to your psyche. It can make you question if there is something wrong with you. Then you may experience additional guilt as you think about what others may think of your children. The complexities of parenting can leave you feeling bewildered.

Fortunately, God specializes in loving anybody and everybody. He's given us example after example of loving and accepting all manner of people. Lepers, He healed them. Tax collectors, He dined with them. Accusers, He forgave them. God not only accepts them, He calls out for them to come to Him. Do your children know that they can come to you, just as they are and that you'll love and accept them? Do you just as readily accept your child with a learning difference as you do with your child that learns easily? Do you accept your daughter who'd much rather wear sweatpants and sneakers than dresses? Do you accept that your son has zero interest in sports?

While loving unconditionally is difficult and truly requires the help of the Holy Spirit to carry out, acceptance may be even harder. When I think of my children, bone of my bone, flesh of my flesh, oh, how I love my children deeply. To share the close, inextricable bond of having carried a child in your womb knits you together in a way that is almost beyond comprehension. Their differences, hmm, not so much. Differences can be hard to understand. I think most of us secretly pray that our children come out perfect with no abnormalities and no differences. While we envision they will be great leaders and stand out, we want them to stand out in ways that are palatable and easy to accept. Stand out as an all-star athlete; don't stand out the sensitive boy. Stand out as the Valedictorian; don't stand out for your Tourette's ticks.

Was it easy for me to accept that one of my children has to make noise in order to learn? No! In fact, initially, I tried to fight it. I wanted this one to be like me, to learn like me. I wanted this child to sit QUIETLY and to sit still and to do her work already. Initially, I tried to force this child to comply with my way of learning. This made a time that should have been enjoyable quite frustrating for us both. Once I accepted that this was merely part of the way this child was wired, I adapted my approach. I also had to advocate for my child in school because not all of her teachers recognized that she is a musical-rhythmic learner. Many years have transpired since then and this child still taps and hums as she works. And this child also happens to excel academically.

Acceptance sees through the eyes of God.

Acceptance sees through the eyes of faith.

Jesus has taken a bit of himself and placed it in our children. Jesus said the kingdom of God belongs to such as these (children) so when we look into the faces of our children we get to see a glimpse of Jesus. Let us not be so busy doing for them that we miss being with them and miss an opportunity to connect with the Jesus in them. And connecting with the Jesus in them is accepting them for who HE created them to be.

There are many promises declared for those who love the Lord: protection, provision, mercy, grace, the kingdom, and blessing beyond what we can think or imagine. God didn't give us all these promises for us to keep for ourselves. I can only conclude then that we are expected to pass on the love and to share the provision. Keep in mind, you are a conduit, not a cul-de-sac of love. In accepting our children for who He created them to be, you pave the way to transfer God's blessing to them.

Rejecting our children can impede our ability to transfer blessings to them. In repeatedly telling children about the differences, shortcomings or harping on habits that you just don't like, you close the door to intimacy with them. Then when it comes time to speak words of affirmation, encouragement, or blessings, they may be leery to receive. And it can be something as simple as saying to your son, "You're slow", "Hurry up. Why are you always working so slow?", "Will you ever learn how to hurry up?". With these words, you've told this child that the way they move is not okay. Acceptance says we embrace and even celebrate individuals who are deliberate, purposeful, and careful. Remember the tortoise.

We don't want to see Jesus face-to-face and have to answer for how we missed an opportunity to connect with Him by connecting with our children. Just the same, we don't want to miss an opportunity to connect hearts with our children all because we can't get over ourselves and accept them the way they are. Since all of God's children are made in His image, when we look into the eyes of our children, we should see the God in them. Peer deeply into their faces, staring intently. Can you see Him there? He's staring back at you with eyes of love. If you look at your children and are filled with something other than acceptance, I pray that He opens the eyes of your heart and the eyes of your understanding so that you can see Him staring back at you in the faces of your children.

. . . .

PRACTICAL APPLICATION

This week, make it a habit to show your love through direct eye contact. Come into close proximity when speaking to your child. Be mindful to keep the face and eyes soft and full of love when engaging with them.

. . . .

prayer

*Out of your unfailing love for me God,
you sent your Son to die for me and for that I
say thank you. Through your example of everlasting love, I am empowered to love. Open the
eyes of my heart so that I see, love and accept
my children as they are. Where there is a heart
of stone, remove it and give me a heart of flesh.
Let me be a conduit not cul-de-sac of love and
let me always remember that love never fails.
You, God, are the embodiment of love and
YOU never fail. You never fail me and you
never fail my children.*

⇌

Chapter 5

AGES AND STAGES

*When I was a child, I spoke like a child, I
thought like a child, I reasoned like a child.
When I became a man, I gave up childish
ways. 1 Corinthians 13:11*

HAVE YOU EVER DEALT WITH an emotional moody teenager?
What about a ten-year old that tries to reason with you about
everything? How about a stubborn, willful three-year old who
refuses to let you help them get dressed? Welcome to the club.
These common occurrences are a natural part of child development. As children undergo physiological changes, the impact
will be seen and felt in day-to-day life. When you embrace this
as a normal, healthy part of growing up, you are more apt to not
be caught by surprise, to not take their behavior as a personal

attack against you, and to not question what you're doing wrong. Instead, you are fully aware of what to expect at each age and stage of development. Just as Jesus has lovingly walked you through different stages of maturity, you will walk hand in hand with your children as they navigate unfamiliar terrain.

Just when you think you've got it all figured out, parenting throws you for a loop. You've finally figured out the terrible twos. In fact, they weren't really that terrible. You enjoyed watching your little baby grow up and engage in eloquent conversation, and then here comes the trying threes. Now your sweet little talker is all about, "I do it by myself". Up until this point, you've taken charge to do everything for them; now, they are exerting independence. What?!

Just when you think you know what life is like having a boy child, you welcome another man-child who is different than your other son. This one is the alpha. He stands on your dining room table, talking loudly as if he's giving The State of the Union Address. Just when you think you know what life is like having a little girl, you get a little girl who doesn't like tights and who likes all things sports. Then, just because we think we've got it all figured out, we get thrown for a huge loop when our previously sweet compliant child begins to negate everything we say. Parenting will keep you clinging fiercely to the old rugged cross. Help me Jesus!

Just as there are natural cycles and rhythms in creation, God's most beautiful creation, humans, follow cycles and rhythms. There is a pacing to our children's development. The quicker we are to recognize this and to catch the wave, the better equipped we are to love them through their evolution. And it takes the help of the Holy Spirit to assess what phase our children are in. While there are some common stages based on age, those are just estimates as every child is unique in the way they've been fashioned. And chronological age is just an estimate as children grow and mature at different rates. In his book, *Romancing Your Child's Heart,* Monty Swan likens a child's heart to a garden, stating the soil needs to be cultivated and that the timing must be right. He says if we aren't careful, we run the risk of trying to plant seeds in soil that is untilled and not fertile.[7]

If we are not acutely aware of where our children are developmentally, we run the risk of parenting out of sync. From my observation, I see many moms and dads parenting from stages that are either ahead of or behind the child's development. Some parents unknowingly accelerate where they think a child should be emotionally. Some parents are slow on the take and are babying an adolescent. Parenting from the right stage empowers us to address issues timely and proactively as opposed to reactively. Do you want to pick your third grader up from school one day to have them blindside you with, "Dad, what is SEX?" Dead silence in the car. He spoke not a word. Poor dad.

Frolicking and playing, each spring, Bambi and family comes frolicking through my yard. The babies usually come in a pair. Carmel colored with a smattering of white spots, these babies are so cute. But never far away is mama deer. When the children are very young, the babes stay very close. They hover near her back legs (close to the source of nourishment as that's where her udders are). They stray a foot or two away at most, looking around, ears perked, heads darting back and forth, but always under mama's watchful eye. As they get older, more and more distance is given between where they play and where mama stands. Still keeping a watchful eye, she gives them space to graze and play. From a distance of 4-5 feet now, mama continues to keep a watchful eye on her babies. Well, now its autumn. Those babies have grown up. The siblings are still together, but mama is out of sight. Let's learn from Bambi. She interacts differently with her children as they move through their ages and stages of development. So, let us walk through the ages.

0-5

What an exciting few years packed with tremendous growth and development. From learning to hold one's head up, to being able to verbally communicate thoughts and emotions, the development during these years is astounding. It just takes my breath away. And the old adage, "enjoy it while you can because these years fly by" is very true.

In the infancy stage, though fraught with sleepless nights and sometimes unexplainable cries, meeting the needs of the baby are pretty straightforward: fed in a timely manner, kept warmed and comforted, nurtured, kept dry, and soothed, baby will generally be content. In the early years, some may find it relatively easy to parent. While it can be challenging to know why a baby is inconsolable, there are generally a few reasons why and most have a pretty easy fix. That becomes more complicated as they grow and mature. The early years are primarily meeting temporal needs, while showing love and affection. But moving into the years of youth gets tricky. So, let's relish this phase where hugs are usually limitless, laughs are plentiful and learning is explosive.

In this stage, children generally communicate and connect through emotion. So, don't be shocked at temper tantrums. Don't be surprised when a child is delightfully content one minute and weepy the next. Seek to make an emotional connection with your child. It tickles me to see parents try to use reason and logic with a three-year old. What the child needs is not a well-thought out discourse on managing their emotions; they may just need a hug. Logic cannot address emotion. Only emotion can temper emotion. Wherever they are emotionally, meet them in that space. Show genuine concern and empathy. This will help your child feel loved and secure.

Why on earth are so many pre-schoolers sitting down in classrooms most of the day? At this stage, children mostly learn through play. And by play, I'm not talking about something that has a battery. I'm talking about old-fashioned play; you know; dress up, play family, imaginary friends. How about puzzles, wooden blocks, play dough and sock puppets? Let us be intentional in creating environments conducive to playing. Not only at Chuck E. Cheese's but home should be a place where a kid can be a kid.

AUTHORITY

From birth to about age five, in addition to establishing a foundation of love and security, you, the parent, establish yourself as the authority figure. God created the entire universe in an orderly fashion. And every facet of life finds itself within the parameters of authority. We must subject ourselves under God, to the laws of the land and to a boss. The Lord expects the parent to assume this rightful position as authority in the home. It is from this position that the child learns to subject themselves unto the parents as they are being shaped to subject themselves under God. Learning to honor the position of authority begins in the home and will serve to bless your children for the rest of their lives.

Depending on your own experiences with authority figures, you may shirk at the use of the word and its implications. So, let me be clear here. When I'm talking about authority, I am NOT talking about controlling children's lives, bossing people around, or being a parent bully. Neither am I talking about passively letting our parenting run its own course. I'm talking about being the lead influencer in your child's life. I'm talking about being a covering and protection for your child. Many problems that we see in the world today can be attributed to a lack of submission to authority. Parents, we must take back our rightful place, not abusing the position or neglecting the position with passivity but by standing firm in the position so that our children will grow up recognizing and respecting the role of authority.

Adherence to this structure is for the child's benefit and blessing. The first command with a promise states,

Children, obey your parents in the Lord, for this is right. "Honor your father and mother" (this is the first commandment with a promise), "that it may go well with you and that you may live long in the land." Ephesians 6:1-3.

I recall something my Pastor said that left such a huge impression on me. What he said has stuck with me for nearly 10 years now. He said when engaging with your child, one of you has to be mature and be the adult. That led me to think, if both parent and child are having a temper tantrum, what would get accomplished? If both parent and child are in a battle of wills, who will win the power struggle? Remember your position of authority, and take your rightful place as executive of the home. Your children will be all the better for it both today and in the long run.

OBEDIENCE

Obedience. Go ahead and let out a sigh; it's okay. It's another one of those words that can rub you the wrong way based on your personal experiences. But under God's authority, there's no way around it. It is a kingdom principle that we are expected to adhere to. And not only should we adhere to it but we should do so willingly. Obedience is doing what is asked of you delightfully and without delay. And like authority, we are training our children to obey us so their hearts are primed to obey God. Teaching children obedience positions them to be able to listen to and obey God's voice. They must learn to be readily obedient to your voice so that they can respond to God's voice when they hear it. When the Lord called out to the child Samuel, Samuel said, "Speak, Lord, your servant is listening" (1 Samuel 3:10). Out of Samuel's obedience to listen and then do as he was told, the scripture goes on to tell us that the Lord was WITH Samuel and none of Samuel's words fell on the ground, Samuel was recognized throughout the land and the Lord continued to reveal himself to him. Isn't that a great promise for your children?

A child's obedience to the parent keeps that child protected under the umbrella of safety. Lack of obedience places a child in harms' way. I saw this played out in a most heart-wrenching way. I was in the late stages of pregnancy and was walking slowly at that point. My three-year old son pulled his hand out of mine and dashed across the parking lot. And wouldn't you know it, a car was backing out. In that flash of a second, the worst picture ran across my mind. Fortunately, the car stopped, but his lack of obedience put him in danger. I had always instructed him to hold my hand in the parking lot and he didn't listen. Obedience is a shield of protection; as such, we want to train our children to stay under its covering.

Obedience is not a feeling but a decision. From a young age, we should teach them to hear and respond accordingly. Even a little baby will turn toward you when you call their name. It starts as simply as that. You train your children to come when they are called, to answer both verbally and to come to you physically. Think about the times the Lord has given you a clear directive and you have not readily complied. I know this case all too well. The Lord has given me a clear message for His people. He has called me to call hearts to OBEDIENCE. But I have to admit, even in writing this book, I was slow to obey. And guess what? Slow to obey = no obey. This is painful to admit. I am downright embarrassed because one of the three pillars my ministry is built on is obedience and here I was SLOW to write. I repented and set my hands to do the typing. Now you're holding the book in your hands. Obedience is also devoid of back talk, negotiation, grumbling or complaining.

From chapter 1, we saw that parents have to know the way, go the way, and then show the way. Obedience is not a "Do as I say, not as I do". You are expected to model obedience for them. Do they see you obeying God in your decisions? Do they see you, wife, submitting to your husband? Do they see you honoring your temple by eating right and exercising? You are a portrait of what obedience looks like to them. Let it be a picture worth gazing up. Indeed, obedience is hard. But it's what God expects of you and what you expect of your children. *Why do you call me, 'Lord, Lord', and do not do what I say? Luke 6:46*

We do not obey because it's easy or because we feel like it. We obey because it's what God requires of us. We obey because it's the least we can do in response to all that God has done for us. We obey because we love God. A friend of mine says obedience is God's love language. Won't you show him you love him by being obedient? Your obedience will leave an indelible mark on the hearts of your children, compelling them to live their lives in surrender and obedience to the Lord. In training our children to obey, remember to extend grace, knowing that even for us obedience is not easy. Obedience is in direct opposition to our willful nature. Continue to redirect their hearts back to doing what's right. Each time we lovingly redirect their hearts, we're helping them be better positioned to readily heed the voice of the Lord.

LITTLE PEOPLE IN THEIR OWN RIGHT

I was shopping in a grocery store where you have to bag your own groceries. As I was bagging, one of my children was just talking, talking, talking. Now this child has the gift of gab. In fact, he talks almost non-stop and that's no exaggeration. Well, this day was no exception. Couple the talking with whining as he was cranky from having had shots earlier in the day, and you had a recipe for a mama ready to stick her head in the sand. And though I was silently thinking, I wish he would be quiet, I gently responded to his unceasing chatter. When his talking becomes overbearing and I'm on the verge of telling him to be quiet, I remember my sweet friend whose son is in speech therapy. It brings into perspective then that my son's chatter is not a clamor but a sweet melody.

The woman next to me bagging her groceries said, *"I've been watching you with your son. You've been so patient with him. It's like I forget sometimes that they are little people. They are their own little people with their own thoughts and feelings."* A couple of observations here. First, I didn't know this woman had even been watching us. I had seen her several times in the store but never made direct eye contact with her. Additionally, we never know what impression we're leaving on others. Hence, we should strive to let our light shine so that others see the Father (Matthew 5:16).

Let us remember that while they are children, they are still people in their own right. You may be having a fight with your toddler in the morning because you are still trying to dress them while they insist on dressing themselves. Come on mom, come on dad, the child is quite capable of picking out an outfit and dressing themselves, albeit a mismatched outfit with the pants on crooked but the child has dressed themselves nonetheless. As they would say, I'm A Big Kid Now.

It is said that by age five, we are who we are. By this age, the overall personality is established. And personality is not just shaped by one's environment; our genes also help form our personality. Because personality is partly informed by biology, it will not drastically change. So, if you've got a five or six-year old, take a good look. Chances are they'll be similar adults. That little person you got to know in this first stage, will bear most of the same characteristics in the next stage with some color added in.

6-11

While the primary influence in the first stage of development is the parent, the primary influence now shifts to others: peers, friends, teachers, and coaches. During this stage, their personalities continue to emerge. Children want to exercise their right to choose. They also want to express their individuality. I saw this in one of my children this year. In previous years, she had enjoyed sharing her birthday with her brother, as their birthdays are three days apart. Even though they are two years apart, we jokingly call them twins because they are the best of friends. So, I was slightly taken aback when she asked to please not share her birthday. Indeed, her need for individuality surfaced. And we honored her request.

Friendships become more important in this stage. Children begin thinking more closely about friends. They examine how to choose a friend. They think about who would make a suitable friend and why. They can experience rejection from a friend. They get a taste of being friends today, not friends tomorrow, and then back together the day after.

Children in this stage begin embracing that there's a whole world that exists outside their home. They begin to see the world beyond themselves. They may seek out opportunities to connect with friends by going to the friend's house. One of my children was chomping at the bit to get to a friend's house. Faithfully, every weekend he would ask, "Whose house can I go over?" The first time I allowed him to attend a birthday party without me, I dropped him off at a classmate's house. I actually left him there for 3 hours. The Lord really had to help me with that one. While my mind was racing a mile a minute with worry about him, I bet his thoughts were just fun, fun, fun.

While it was a challenge for me to "release" him and let him attend the party without me present, it was a natural and necessary action for this stage of development. He was 10 years old after all. My hesitation in leaving him was not because I was concerned about his welfare; I was just stuck in the prior stage of development. But that was a necessary step as it led to the next step, which was attending a weeklong overnight scouting camp. Part of this stage calls for our children to develop a sense of responsibility. This can be reinforced in having chores, keeping up with school assignments and taking care of personal items. How will they have an opportunity to exercise and show responsibility if they never have to practice it because we are hand holding? Parents, as you move through this stage, gone are the days of babying. I am not saying they are autonomous. They are still walking right beside you.

Another very important development in this stage is the continued growth of gross motor skills. They become more adept and more agile with their bodies. Think about what recess looks like for kids in kindergarten through sixth grade. Most children like to run, jump, and move. Their bodies have tons of energy that need to be expended. So, create time for them to get out and play. Today's culture would have our children spend exorbitant amounts of time plugged into devices. Let's ditch the devices and get their bodies moving. I've got one child who is not inclined to play outside but I make sure he gets out there too.

Additionally, issues of the heart arise in this stage and we are presented with plenty of opportunities to shape character. We'll be discussing Character Development at length in chapter 7. In the latter part of this stage, most begin approaching puberty. They also begin to use logic reasoning. Parents will we provide space for choice, individuality, responsibility, and character shaping or will we tightly restrict, treating them as if they're the young children from stage 1? Remember, one of the biggest pitfalls in parenting is to engage your child for a prior stage of development.

12-18

Okay parents, I'm going to ask you to get quiet and still for a minute. Scan through the card catalog of your mind and find the call numbers for the books on your teen years. Grab those books off the shelf and leaf through the pages. What do you see? Think about the friends you had. Recall what you looked like. What changes did you experience in your body? Did you like your hair? What kinds of clothes did you wear? What were you embarrassed about? What boy/girl did you have a crush on? Who bullied you? What did you cry about? Who did you dislike? What made you happy? Did anyone prepare you for puberty or were you left to figure it out on your own?

I want you to sit in that emotion for a minute. Let it ALL become as fresh for you today as it was then. It is from that place that I encourage you to connect with your child who is in this stage. Out of the three stages addressed here, I believe this one is the most fragile and requires a delicate hand. What I see from many parents is quite the opposite. What I find is that parents' expectations of their children during this stage are way too high. We miss that their brains are still developing and that they are not cognitively mature enough to always make sound choices. We can forget the emotional turmoil they are experiencing as a result of hormonal changes.

This stage sees our children grappling with so much at one time. They question their identity. They tend to seek out peer groups as a means of establishing an identity. They question, "Who am I?" While they want to exert their independence, part of them longs to still feel connected to home life. So, we see some children detach, wanting to spend more time alone in their rooms; they may "hide" in their hoodie sweatshirts, shirking away from the world. Oh, the delicate balance we must have in giving them space yet engaging them in family life.

The physical changes are the easiest to pinpoint because they smack us right in the face. One day you're holding your sweet little one in your lap. The next day you go to hug your child and you notice you are hugging at eye level. Your son now has hairy legs. Dad, you go to hug your baby girl and she has boobs. Whoa, that's awkward. With those physical changes come intense emotions and bouts of moodiness and crying can seemingly erupt out of the blue. Poor kids! What they need most during this phase is empathy, wrapped up in compassion and understanding. Even though they think they know it all, they don't but they don't know that.

We even see Mary and Joseph struggle with this as their pre-adolescent son asserted His independence. *Every year Jesus' parents went to Jerusalem for the Festival of the Passover. When he was twelve years old, they went up to the festival, according to the custom. After the festival was over, while his parents were returning home, the boy Jesus stayed behind in Jerusalem, but they were unaware of it. Thinking he was in their company, they traveled on for a day. Then they began looking for him among their relatives and friends. When they did not find him, they went back to Jerusalem to look for him. After three days they found him in the temple courts, sitting among the teachers, listening to them and asking them questions. Everyone who heard him was amazed at his understanding and his answers. When his parents saw him, they were astonished. His mother said to him, "Son, why have you treated us like this? Your father and I have been anxiously searching for you." "Why were you searching for me?" he asked. "Didn't you know I had to be in my Father's house?" But they did not understand what he was saying to them. Then he went down to Nazareth with them and was obedient to them. But his mother treasured all these things in her heart. And Jesus grew in wisdom and stature, and in favor with God and man. Luke 2:41-52*

While gone are the days of hand holding, the same level of delicate care and compassion that you had for a newborn still serves a great purpose in this stage. This is not babying but living out the fruit of the spirit of patience, gentleness, and kindness.

But we were gentle among you, just as a nursing mother
cherishes her own children. 1 Thessalonians 2:7

They need you mom. They need you dad. They need you grandparents. They are under tremendous pressure. Pressure from peers, pressure from teachers, pressure to fit in, pressure to stand out, pressure to perform, hey, even pressure from you! They are listening to you. They care about what you think. They just want to make you proud. They love you, they really do. Love them back by being open, accessible, non-critical and non-judgmental.

ADULTHOOD

You know what typically happens here; one of two things. The parent with the "18 and you're out" mindset has dropped the kid like a hot potato. You're on your own; I've done my part, so figure it out is their way of proceeding with the parent/child relationship. Or the other extreme treats the adult child as if they're still a kid. The parent is still telling their child what to do. That parent that is still managing all the child's affairs. This is really a stage where we can clearly see parents stuck in how to relate to and engage with their children.

I mentioned previously that I raised my sister in her early teen through early adult years. Our mother died when we were young and it had been my desire since I was 18 to have her with me. With the loving support of my husband, after we purchased our first home, she came to live with us. After being with us for about six years, she went to live on her own. After she left, there was a period of adjustment in our relationship. I think she thought I'd still be trying to tell her what to do with her life (perhaps I did a time or two). I felt she then kept her distance because she didn't want to hear it. I came to accept that she was an adult, and I would no longer tell her what to do. I accepted that my role had shifted from telling to advising, from doing to listening. Instead of always offering my two cents, I began to simply ask open-ended questions as prompts to get her thinking things through. And the result? She began to open up more. I'm happy with where we are today. As adults, we have mutual respect for one another. As your children move through their ages and stages, be diligent to be patient, loving, kind, gracious and merciful. You'll all fare better because of it. Here are a few power plays to assist you in moving through the ages and stages.

POWER PLAYS

SPEAK LIFE

Life and death are in the power of the tongue. Can your words to your children serve as their playlist? If I were to go on your child's phone and play the playlist MOM, what words would I hear? What would I hear from you, DAD? When they were young, you were so careful to guard them from certain TV shows, music, bad language, etc., but would your words on repeat be much different? Would the playlist of your words minister life or death, blessing or cursing?

"Sticks and stones can break my bones, but words can never hurt me". When called a name, we would retort with, "I know you are but what am I?" "I'm rubber, you're glue, whatever you say bounces off of me and sticks to you!" These childhood phrases we used to say are false. Words do hurt. Words do matter. Words do stick. So, make sure your words to your children speak life. Make sure your words speak truth. When you talk, your children may seem aloof at times, but your words are impacting them.

I've taught my children that words bless or burn; they heal or hurt. Words are not neutral. Every word does something. Think about words that were said to you or about you. From a relative, friend, teacher or parent. Many of these words help shape the adult you are today. You may even still be suffering from the damage inflicted by these words. So, use your mouth to bless. To bless is to speak well of. Jacob blessed each of his 12 children with a blessing unique to the individual (Genesis 49:28). Over them, speak words of affirmation and encouragement. Speak words that offer hope and healing. Lift up words of comfort in times of fear or distress. Proclaim who God says they are.

HAVE FAITH

Every decision we make is rooted in either love or fear. From deciding who we'll allow to babysit our children to supporting which college they'll attend, the decisions are based on our sense of security or lack thereof. Take for example the parents' reaction to seeing their innocent little three-year old daughter dancing. The parent looks upon this sweet little girl, dancing her heart out. She's feeling the music and rocking and swaying in sheer wonder. Then comes a slight roll of the hips. The parent immediately turns off the music, holds the child by the shoulders and exclaims, "Don't you dare dance like that!" The poor sweet girl has no idea what's just happened.

Or take the example of the five-year-old son. He's got a seven-year-old sister who loves baby dolls. These two siblings are best friends and playmates to the end. So, when his sister asks him to play baby dolls together, he delightfully agrees. She plays mommy, he plays daddy and they care for their baby. Dad comes upon the scene and sternly reprimands his son saying, "No son, you will NOT play with dolls! Boys don't do that."

What do we see happening here? Fear-based parenting. The parent in the first scenario sees their precious little girl moving her hips. Their thoughts run away, a thousand miles a minute. In their mind, she has rolled those hips all the way up to being 15 and pregnant.

The dad allowed his thoughts to run away with him too. He sees his son 19 and gay. Fear is a strong motivator often compelling people to make irrational decisions. But be reminded; we have not been given a spirit of fear. When rearing our children, we have to continually redirect our thoughts back to the truth. And the truth says perfect love casts out fear (1 John 4:18). When engaging with your children, if you find yourself overreacting to a situation, use that as a prompt to pause and do some self-reflection, asking yourself, "Am I reacting to this out of love or fear?" If it is fear, follow that up by asking yourself, "What am I afraid will happen to my child?" Then find an applicable bible truth to shed light on your fear. Perfect love gives fear its marching orders (1 John 4:18).

By the way, as I was leaving a spirited evening of high worship during our church's annual women's conference, who would I see walking up the aisle? The woman from the grocery store. It was so crowded, I'm surprised I was able to make her out in the crowd. Something in me said catch up with her. I ran up the aisle and out into the halls and gently tapped her on the arm. She turned, gave me a smile, then did the *hum, I recognize you but I don't know from where* look. I thanked her for giving me the bags a few days ago. She paused then said, *"You go here {To First Baptist}? No wonder you are so patient."* As if saying, yes, you are living out the Word we receive here and it was evident in the way you interacted with your child. We are always on display for God.

PRACTICAL APPLICATION

Do an activity with your child of their choosing. The mall, coloring or even building forts; it's their choice. This is your opportunity to enter their world. While engaging with your child, tell him a story about when you were a kid.

prayer

Father, You are the same yesterday, today and forever more. From everlasting to everlasting you are good and your mercy endures forever. I thank you for walking alongside me as I guide my children through their ages and stages of development. You are a God of divine timing. And there is a time and place for everything under the heavens. Allow me to walk in time with my children, neither parenting ahead nor behind where they are physically, emotionally, mentally or spiritually. Let me walk in perfect sync with them. Allow your spirit at work in me to remain tenderhearted toward them on days their behavior makes them unlovable. Just as you love me in each stage I find myself, let me extend that same grace and mercy to my children. Lord, I thank you that my children continue to thrive, reaching their maximum potential as you have preordained.

~

Chapter 6

WHAT ABOUT DISCIPLINE?

Train up a child in the way he should go,
and when he is old he will not depart from it.
Proverbs 22:6

CHILDREN ARE A HECK OF a lot of fun but let's face it; much of their behavior can be downright disagreeable. They can lie, pester, whine, annoy and just outright frustrate you. As a parent, it takes maturity to have patience and self-control when instructing and redirecting our children's hearts. And that maturity enables us to artfully dole out discipline that is rooted in love. Out of the Lord's love, He disciplines and as parents, we are to do the same.

My son, do not despise the Lord's discipline, and do not resent his rebuke, because the Lord disciplines those he loves, as a father the son he delights in. Proverbs 3:11-12

When I use the word discipline, what immediately comes to your mind? Depending on your frame of reference, some may think of the rod, others may think of exercise, someone else may think of prayer. Discipline is actually the *practice of training* someone to follow a particular set of rules or code of conduct. Discipline comes from the Latin root word for pupil, which is *discipulus*. The Latin word, *disciplina,* means instruction given, teaching, or learning. Going a step further, *discere* means to learn. So, before we go any further into the process of how we discipline, we must back track to ensure we've established a firm foundation on which to stand when administering discipline. You can't take money out of the bank unless you've made a deposit and the same can be said when disciplining. You cannot effectively discipline unless you've already established an environment of love and acceptance, as addressed in Chapter 4.

Let me say here, I used to think discipline meant punishment and correction. If discipline then is the practice of training, I don't believe it has to always come about through punishment, chastisement and suffering but more so through modeling, direct instruction, and coaching. If you'd seen the earlier version of this chapter, it would have told a different story. But that's the wondrous beauty of the God we serve. When we ask for wisdom, He doles it out liberally. He opens the eyes of our understanding. And He's given me a fresh, unbiased, unfiltered look at this subject. My old view was somewhat distorted. So, permit me if you will, to share with you the view with the veil removed. I'm going to ask you to lay aside preconceived notions and how you were disciplined. Together, let's take a fresh look.

Jesus systematically disciplined the disciples. That's why they are called disciples. They were pupils of the Master. And at His feet, they received discipline. Remember the definition from above, instruction. Jesus modeled for us through his interactions with the disciples what discipline looks like. He did what I mentioned in chapter 1, *know the way, go the way, and then show the way*. He told them, this is what I do. They observed Him doing what He told them. He gave them an opportunity to put His teachings into practice. Then He released them to do it on their own.

We also see this model occur in the classroom. Teachers, back me up on this. When the teacher is introducing a new concept, he or she starts by giving a direct instruction. The teacher may stand in the front of the class at the whiteboard (gone are the days of blackboards and chalk) and walk step by step through the problem. The teacher will then address questions, after which they will do guided practice. Here, the teacher will shift from direct teaching to facilitating. The teacher will call upon a particular student or request a volunteer. Then students may work collaboratively with peers. Here, the teacher is watching and observing the students. The teacher may give praise, provide clarity, or prompt. Lastly, the students will have an opportunity to work independently to show mastery of the subject matter.

Parents, we often RUSH the process. We want to move from direct instruction to independent practice in a single bound. And the teachers will tell you that a great deal of time may be spent in the guided practice mode. Don't miss this or else you'll find yourself feeling like you're going backwards again and again. Give time for practice before you expect mastery.

Do any of your children play an instrument? Do you expect to move a squeaky recorder player to a first chair flutist in one step? No. Discipline is a PROCESS. And as such, it takes time. And because it takes time, you can expect to cover some of the same areas again and again. Look at how often the word says you'll be instructing.

These commandments that I give you today are to be on your hearts. Impress them on your children. Talk about them when you sit at home and when you walk along the road, when you lie down and when you get up. Tie them as symbols on your hands and bind them on your foreheads. Deuteronomy 6:6-8

Yup. That pretty much amounts to all day every day. And even when you're not directly instructing, your child has tied your words to their hands and in their heads so your instruction is with them even if you don't immediately see the fruit of it. And if you are not seeing the fruit, don't lose heart. Depending on the variety, it can take an apple tree between two to seven years to bear viable fruit. Your children are listening and they will bear fruit.

Whoever gives heed to instruction prospers, and blessed is the one who trusts in the LORD. Proverbs 16:20

Remember this; Discipline = Instruction

I've said it in previous chapters but, hey, I'm going to say it again. It begins with modeling. Remember, it starts with you. You know the way, so go the way. That means you walk the talk. Additionally, when instructing, *learning* is the goal not control. This one hit me personally like an anvil falling on my head. When my first-born was young, she was an easy student for me to teach. She sat compliantly, actively engaged with me and was eager to learn. When I began teaching my first-born son, it was a different story. After circle time, he seemed to check out. He was more apt to crawl on the floor, stand on the table or crumple his papers. One day, we were working on the letter A. I was determined for him to sit still and trace all of these A's. He got up from the dining table and walked to a nearby coffee table. When I finished helping his sister, I went over to get him. I was irritated and was intent on putting him back in that seat to write those A's. But wouldn't you know. On the back of his paper were a bunch of neat letter N's. In that moment, God asked me, "Are you trying to teach or trying to control?" My efforts to teach had morphed into control. I wanted him to do it my way and no other way. The encounter left an indelible impression on me and radicalized how I approach instructing my children.

If we go back to the premise that discipline is instruction, what then should we spend our time instructing? The home is the training ground for principles, character and conviction. It has been demonstrated that children in schools with character education perform better academically and experience reduced behavior issues.[8] If character training has that much impact in the school environment, imagine the fantastic results discipline yields when administered in the home by loving parents?

All our instruction and training is done to build their muscle as to become internally motivated. We long for them to make decisions for themselves, based on their values and beliefs. We want them to be able to hold firm to their convictions, being able to clearly differentiate right from wrong. We don't want them making decisions solely because Dad or Mom said so. It has to come from some place deeper. Rest assured the day will come when they have to decide. We will not always be around and we want them to choose well. Sometimes parents offer external motivators. Some dangle the carrot (promise of reward) or the stick (threat of penalty). Doing so runs counter to exercising conviction. When we use the stick or the carrot, we stand right between them and conviction.

If people are good only because they fear punishment, and hope for reward, then we are a sorry lot indeed. ~ *Albert Einstein*

CORRECTION

'Tis the nature of the beast. Since childhood is a time filled with self-discovery and learning, mistakes are bound to happen. And the home is a safe place for our children to make mistakes. It is under our covering that we can lovingly provide correction. Godly correction is dispensed not to be vengeful or spiteful but to help our children reach their full potential. *Because the Lord disciplines the one he loves, and he chastens everyone he accepts as his son. Hebrews 12:6*

Many of the major car brands today are using automatic braking technology. The cars use radars, cameras or lasers to detect a potential collision. This technology has the ability to prevent a deadly collision or at least lessen the effects. You are to function in the same way. You are the radar that keeps them safe, sparing them from potentially fatal collisions. You engage the brakes by guiding their hearts back to God when they are approaching danger. You do that by taking them by the hand and leading them back to God's principles. With young children, that will often mean literally taking them by the hand and steering them in the opposite direction. For older children, it may mean showing them the end result of the dangerous activity or behavior.

For every word of correction, do you share a word of love? Is a word given that says even though I'm not pleased with the behavior, you are still loved, valued, appreciated? When working as a corporate trainer, I learned a coaching technique called the sandwich. When giving corrective feedback, we were raged to sandwich the correction between affirmations. also called it the 1-1-2. We would say one affirmation, one correction and conclude with two affirmations.

RESPOND VS. REACT

When instructing, it is important to respond versus react. To respond is to pause and think. It is to take a pregnant pause. In that pregnant pause, God has the ability to lengthen time. Though but a brief moment, God will give you the ability to assess a situation, check in with your own emotion and respond in love. During the pregnant pause, ask yourself is what I'm about to say or do going to escalate or diffuse the situation? Just ask Him to freeze the frame while you think it through. He is faithful to deliver. To react is to act on impulse and to be led by your emotion. When your child dropped her whole plate of dinner, did you fly off the handle? Was your comeback commensurate with the offense? Sure; spilled food is messy but a response not a reaction would be appropriate here.

After getting the mail out of the mailbox, I made the trek back down my very long driveway. I saw one of my children approaching and he was not empty handed. The five- year old was carrying the two-month old! Like Rafiki holding up Simba in The Lion King, big brother continued walking toward me. My frantic mommy mind played out the whole scene. My sweet newborn splattered on the blacktop, shrieking in terror. Yes, I could see it clearly. But in that pause, God lengthened time. Rapid fire, He told me to capture those toxic thoughts. He told me big brother is just trying to help out. And He told me to calmly coach big brother to hold on tight and to stand still until I reached him. My driveway seemed extra long that day. But responding in love and not reacting out of emotion saved us a trip to the E.R. Had I reacted, I feel he would have surely dropped the baby. Another tool that can help us to respond vs. react is to judge the intent. During that pregnant pause, ask yourself, what is their intent. In this scenario, his intent was to be a helper to me and to be a big brother to the baby.

BEHAVIOR

Behavior is merely a communication vehicle. It's your child's way of conveying they need you. You are the one they rely on. You are the one they trust. So, it is you they turn to for solutions to their problems. And because of their lack of maturity (as covered in Chapter 5), they have yet to acquire the skills to clearly articulate what they're thinking and feeling. So, it manifests as behavior. They are looking for reassurance that you see, that you love and that you care. So, when you witness behavior that is unbecoming, don't be sidetracked by it. As my friend says, address the behavior; do not attack the child.

When a child cannot handle a situation, they tend to act out in a big way. And that is completely understandable. Remember, they only have (insert your child's age) years of life experience to draw on. You have (insert your age) years of experience to draw upon when responding to situations. And to think, with the breadth of experience you have, there are times you too respond inappropriately. So, imagine how difficult it is for a young child. All they know is how frustrated they are. Their behavior is trying to communicate to you that they are frustrated and need your help to solve the problem. The bible says, "God is a very present help in the time of trouble" (Psalm 46:1). When your children are in distress, will you be a very present help or will you shut them down because they are having a hard time managing their emotions?

Speak the behavior you want to see. Look for opportunities to recognize good behavior and affirm the small steps they've taken to improve. Put yourself in the child's place. Remember the boss scenario from the previous chapter? Everyone needs encouragement, even you and all the more so with developing children. Instill a sense of personal responsibility by giving the child room to make decisions or to be a part of the decision-making process. Keep in mind, behavior does not change overnight but like a tender sapling, it needs delicate tending.

Have your child visualize what they want to accomplish and, together, strategize a plan to reach the goal. One of my children had a goal to enter the National Junior Honor Society. Together, we strategized a plan to get there. It was a great motivator for him. And as his parent, it gave me something to reference when he complained about schoolwork or was not giving it his all. Once again, don't forget about the power of modeling. Do your children see you motivated? Do they see you set goals? Do you share with them your struggles and successes in reaching goals? Your personal stories will help it become even more tangible for them. I'm striving to meet my personal goals and so is my son. National Junior Honor Society, here he comes.

NATURAL CONSEQUENCES

Natural consequences are naturally occurring results of your child's behavior. Just as there are natural laws that govern the universe, our children need to know that natural consequences will flow from their decisions. It's a life lesson of cause and effect. It is a powerful life lesson for your children to learn early on that if I do this action, this will be the result. And letting children face the consequences of their choices shouldn't begin in adulthood but should happen first within the context of the home.

Parents, I know it's hard for you to stand back and watch your children fail. I know it's difficult to stand on the sideline and witness your children hurt. But trying to spare them from every possible eventuality does them a greater disservice. Can you remember meeting someone perhaps in college or on one of your first "real" jobs that had never experienced life because their parents were still doing a great deal of hand holding? Some of them had never been the beneficiaries of owning natural consequences and consequently, they had a harder time adjusting to real life. So, Mom, your 6th grader didn't turn in a month's work of homework. Do you badger the teacher demanding that he be allowed to make it up for full credit or do you allow him to accept the grades (bearing in mind you are training your child to be responsible)? The report card reflects your child's proficiency and is not your Purple Heart. Dad, do you contend with the coach for that starting position for your son when you know he's been lazy, hasn't been practicing and, frankly, isn't driven enough to be in the starting line up?

A GREAT lack of natural consequences can be found in the case of the "Affluenza Boy". In 2013, Ethan Couch killed 4 people. Driving drunk and over the speed limit, Couch ended the lives of four people who were stopped along the side of the road trying to assist a driver whose car was disabled. A psychiatrist testified in court that he should not be held liable for the killings because he couldn't comprehend the consequences of his actions, as he had never been held responsible for anything before. The psychiatrist said he suffered from "Affluenza", a product of wealth and privilege by parents who never set limits.[9] Love your children by teaching them responsibility and allowing them to face natural consequences.

DON'TS

Let's cover a couple of the things to avoid. As previously mentioned, we should consistently ask ourselves, "will my words or actions escalate or deescalate the situation?" No need to add fuel to the fire. If you have a child that self-corrects, there's no double jeopardy. There's no need to "make them pay". For some children, their convictions are enough to make them sorrowful for what they've done. Try to refrain from yelling, combativeness, harshness and anger as that just further provokes your child and doesn't help your child solve the problem. Sometimes, parents can abuse the parental role and become bullies. Hitting out of anger, forcing your will upon another and belittling are things we see bullies do. Don't be a bully parent.

Remember your role. Your job is not to be the big bad wolf, to huff and puff and blow the house down. Do you need to prove how big and bad you are and demand to be heard and respected? When you have already established that you are the authority and you are respected, there is no need to swell up. If you feel the need to swell up like a puffer fish, what are you really demonstrating? Those animals puff up to protect themselves from predators. You must then ask yourself, "why do I feel threatened?" There's no need to prove how tough you are. Also, there's no need to over-discipline because you're concerned about what others think. Do not allow what you think others expect of you to influence your parenting. If you think, "My mother will think I let him get away with anything" and over-discipline as a result, that's not fair to the child.

SPANKING

To hit or not to hit, that is the question. For me, the verdict is still out on this one. This is a very polarizing topic. I don't want to draw a line in the sand and separate those that spank from those that don't. Parenting requires community and in community there is mutual love, compassion and understanding. I'm simply sharing where I am currently on this issue. My feelings have evolved over time. So, I will ask you to keep an open heart and to follow the prompting of the Holy Spirit.

The bible is very clear; the rod of correction is a useful tool for administering correction. It is my personal assertion that correction does not take one form. Hence, the rod should not be the sole or the primary methodology for adjusting behavior. When I think about Jesus, sweet Jesus, full of patience, gentleness, kindness, self-control and love, I don't visualize him doling out many spankings. I see a picture of hugging rather than hitting, embracing rather than striking. When I think about Jesus, I see one who would lend a listening ear.

We all know the often-used phrase "spare the rod and spoil the child". This is most likely based on Proverbs 13:24 that says, "He who spares the rod hates his son, but he who loves him is careful to discipline him." When we look more deeply into the word, "rod" in the bible, it is a wooden stick used as a shepherd's staff, a symbol of dominion, a familial branch or tribe, a spear, a stick (used for beating someone), a king's scepter or a tool for measuring. While there are several verses that mention the use of the rod in conjunction with chastisement, we also see it used for comfort and protection. Psalm 23 says with the rod and the staff we are comforted. It is my assessment then, that the rod is not merely a tool for chastisement, but for guidance and redirection. It is not only an instrument that administers pain, but serves as a guide. Thus, it is a component of a greater plan to shape hearts.

Let the Spirit be your guide. Be reminded, the bible encourages us not to provoke them lest they become discouraged but to bring them up in discipline and instruction (Colossians

3:21 and Ephesians 6:4). When you chastise, are you revealing more of Jesus? As a child, I've been the recipient of chastisement doled out in love under self-control and, also, doled out in anger. When I willfully disobeyed my father, he would rarely use the rod of correction. He would calmly share what I had done, then would administer the rod. I had another relative beat me out of her own anger, sometimes for minor infractions I committed but oftentimes with no provocation, simply because she was enraged. Back then, I had strong resentment for the relative who beat me out of her own anger.

The thought of spanking my children makes me uncomfortable. Even when I spank in love, devoid of anger, something in me is unnerved. I have a hard time reconciling in my head hurting a child, even if it is supposedly for their benefit. In my head, I wrestle with the dichotomy of, "I love you, I care for you, I nurture you" but here I am inflicting pain on you. If you don't agree with me here, it's okay; I'm still trying to reckon it in my own head. We can give it fancy names if we want: spank, beat, chastise, flog, pop, whip, discipline, punish, or rod of correction; hitting is still hitting. Have I spanked my children? Yes. Do I feel good about it? No. And it's deeper than the "This hurts me more than it hurts you". We've got biblical justification for spanking. We've got our personal experiences that color how we view spanking. We agree. We disagree. I know this is a tough one.

Whatever your stance, let's try to agree on these few points. Your hands are instruments of love so if administering physical correction, refrain from using your hands. Don't chastise out of your own anger. At the first sight of offense, give a clear command. If offense is repeated, redirection is necessary. This requires you to intervene. Here is where many get lazy. We don't want to stop and directly address the situation. But remember we are not passive parents. We address situations in a timely, head-on manner. And by address, we discuss what happened, then issue any consequences, if applicable. Some consequences may be removing the child from the environment, loss of privileges, a time of reflection, or the rod of correction. Let the Spirit be your guide. Keep it private as to maintain the child's self-worth. Give them an opportunity to repent and, if needed, to make restitution to the offended party. Help them see their offense as unto God.

THE GOAL

Our children are disciples or pupils and we are their primary teachers. Our interactions with them are priming them to be under the tutelage of Christ. Our goal should be to help them rise to the greatness God's deposited in them. We want them to see a picture of their limitless capabilities. We must empower them to own their own success. We must create an environment safe for exploration, learning and for making mistakes. When they do err, we will lovingly steer them back on track.

PRACTICAL APPLICATION

This week, with your new definition of discipline in mind, be patient and purposeful in instructing your children. Identify an area in your child's life that needs additional coaching. Start at the beginning. Explain your expectations. Re-teach if necessary. Allow your child to see how their actions fit into the larger framework of the family and of the kingdom.

prayer

Thank you Lord for giving me the grace to purposefully train my children in the way they should go. I repent for times I've abused my position of leadership and have dealt with my children harshly. Like Jesus, I will be a servant leader who knows the way, goes the way and shows the way. I pray my children will take firm hold of instruction and actively pursue wisdom. My children will not forsake my instruction but will hold it firmly in their heads and in their hearts. When my children act out, I will purpose to remember that their behavior is a cry for help and I will patiently seek to help them. I will rely on the trusted guidance of the Holy Spirit to ensure any correction given is done so in love and not out of my own anger or frustration. I can trust the Holy Spirit to be a very present help as my children and I walk out the process of discipleship.

⪼

Chapter 7

WHAT A CHARACTER!

For we are His workmanship, created in Christ Jesus for good works, which God prepared beforehand that we should walk in them. Ephesians 2:10

WHAT A CHARACTER! WHAT COMES to mind when you hear that euphemism? Maybe you think about the class clown. Perhaps you get an image in your mind of someone who is loud and obnoxious. Whatever comes to mind, we will all be known for something. Character is the distinct quality that makes you…you. Character is the mental and moral makeup of who a person is. If character is the essence of who we are, then it informs what we think and what we think translates into who we will become.

For as he thinks in his heart, so is he Proverbs 23:7a NKJV.

Hence, the job of shaping character is critically important. Genetics may make us more apt to display certain character traits more naturally; others will have to be coached. My sister is naturally patient and compassionate. Me on the other hand, well, not so much. It's something I've had to learn. I am naturally enthusiastic. I've got such an excitement for life that I can't keep it bottled up. Whether natural inclination or coached, our children will be judged by the content of their character.

"Man's character is his fate." Heraclitus

I've heard it said character is what we do when no one is watching. Character surfaces in how we respond to life situations. And we want our children to be able to respond appropriately to whatever situations they may face. Parents, we are character shapers! We are the primary character-molding force in our children's lives. It is our responsibility to help them become the type of people who can change the culture through their influence of honesty, integrity, trustworthiness, compassion, responsibility, decisiveness and more. Since we wield the most influence in our children's lives, we directly and indirectly shape their behavior, attitudes, values and sense of right and wrong.

IN HIS IMAGE

You've got to be over 35 to remember this one. A thin sheet of paper that was coated on one side with blue or black ink, you would slip it between two or more sheets of paper to transfer the image to multiple sheets at once; carbon paper. The carbon paper allowed you to make a duplicate of your original writing. Since we are made in the image of the Father, our character should be reflective of the Creator. Have you ever heard the phrase "You are a carbon copy"? It is generally used to describe someone's physical features.

> *Then God said, "Let Us make man in Our image, according to Our likeness; let them have dominion over the fish of the sea, over the birds of the air, and over the cattle, over all the earth and over every creeping thing that creeps on the earth." So, God created man in His own image; in the image of God He created him; male and female He created them. Genesis 1:26-27.*

You are God's carbon copy. And as such, you are an impression of him. And since your children share your DNA, they are carbon copies too. This is not to suggest they should be or act just like you but that your character should be imitable. While personalities and interests vary, character traits remain. God's character is unchanging. And since we are created in His image, as are our children, we should all reflect His character.

HIS CHARACTER

God reveals His character to us in several ways. Through His actions and through His names, we gain understanding of His character. His word gives us a very clear picture of His character. He is unchanging (Revelation 1:8). He is holy (1 Peter 1:15-16). He is truthful (John 7:28). He is omnipresent (Jeremiah 23:23-24). This is but a small sampling of all that He is. He also reveals his character through His names. Through His names, we get to know El-Roi, the God who sees and who is attentive to our needs. We become acquainted with Jehovah-Raah, the Shepherd who provides gentle guidance and protection. We get to see Jehovah-Sabaoth, the Lord of Hosts who goes before us in battle. He is our defender. And in your own day-to-day living, you get to experience Him personally. If He has healed you, you know Jehovah Rapha. And if He has fought on your behalf and secured the victory, you've gotten to know Jehovah Nissi. This is how we come to know Him most intimately, through His character. And this is how you and your children will be known, through your character.

DEVELOPING CHARACTER

So how is godly character developed? Taking into account our natural proclivity to err and our autopilot responses to lie, cheat, deceive, cover-up, and otherwise sin, our adaptation to godly character starts with right thinking and right believing. This is a prime opportunity to reinforce the need for Jesus as personal Savior and Lord. In our own strength and might, even with our best attempts at being "good", we will fail. It is only by the power of the Holy Spirit that we are able to unveil true Christian character. It is God's transforming power that enables you and your children to consistently show humility, cooperation, generosity and resilience.

Character is often developed through periods of trial and tribulation. God will allow life's pressures to mount. The word *tribulation* literally means "pressure." It is a word that was used to describe crushing grapes in a vat for wine or crushing olives for oil. God wants the oil of gladness to refine your character. He wants to bless you with that which will sustain and give strength, but that sometimes comes about through the pressing. I'm sure you've had a chance to experience life's pressures. Do you allow your children to experience their own pressure and tribulation without running interference every time? These are things God has engineered to build their character.

In the following passage, the word *character* also refers to experience. It is associated with the words tested, proof, and trial. And sometimes it is trial by fire. There will be days our children feel the heat of life circumstances. Perhaps they have a medical issue arise unexpectedly. Maybe they are one of several hundred students trying to enter a competitive school. Sure enough, the heat will be turned up. When precious metals are heated, the impurities rise to the top and are skimmed away, leaving behind a high valuable commodity. The same can be said of our children. When the trials of life heat them up, their exemplary character will remain. *And not only that, but we also*

glory in tribulations, knowing that tribulation produces persever-
ance; and perseverance, character; and character, hope. Now hope
does not disappoint, because the love of God has been poured out
in our hearts by the Holy Spirit who was given to us. Romans 5:1-5

Think of one of the most difficult periods in your life. What character trait did God develop in you through that situation? The same is true for your children. They will have unique character-shaping opportunities. Is it beneficial then to be the helicopter dad, never allowing your child to face any difficulty? I know mom; you want to step in to protect your baby, but facing some trials will be good for them. My first-born is a natural born leader. In most other circles, she is used to being in charge. Currently, she is on a competitive STEM (Science, Technology, Engineering & Math) team. And for the first time ever she was confronted with a situation. There was another young person on the team that was also a natural leader. It was a real challenge for my child to find her place when working with another strong leader. As a parent, some days it was a struggle for me to see my daughter shrink back or to see her pout but I did not intervene because I knew it was building her resilience and tolerance.

How are you equipping your children to pass the tests? Are you giving them room to make mistakes and learn through trial and error? Remember, the home is a learning center and a place safe for making mistakes. And character shaping is often doled out from the hand of adversity. When your children make a mistake, look to maximize on the teachable moment.

Our natural inclination wants to protect and shield our children from hurt. We want to spare them from pain. But we must embrace that their walk is their walk. How will they come to effectively deal with adversity if no adverse situations ever arise? In fact, we'd be doing our children a great disservice if we didn't allow them to experience the breadth of life and that includes pain and disappointment. And we know from personal experience that there is hope on the other side of pain. It brings to mind a song that says, *"There will be glory after this."* So, when our children confront a trial, we don't have to be crushed. We can take joy in knowing they will be victorious.

In the same way Jesus was tested and you and I have been tested, our children will be tested. And how did Jesus respond to the test? He responded with the word of God. What does that show us? He spent time in prayer and He spent time studying the scriptures. His faith was so absolute He knew the Father would sustain Him. Are your children spending time in prayer and spending time in the word so that they will be able to withstand the tests? Ensure that they are duly armed with the word so that they will be able to stand during times of testing.

SHAPING CHARACTER

Our job as character shapers is to continually point our children's hearts toward God. We are to help them keep their thoughts in alignment with God's thoughts, as we want them to have the mind of Christ. In this way, their words, actions, then habits spring from a well of righteousness.

Let this mind be in you which was also in Christ Jesus
Philippians 2:5 NKJV

Character can be shaped through both formal and informal means. Formal character training within the home can be done through family and personal devotions. In what ways are you delving into the word of God as a family? Is it daily during dinner, on the drive to school in the mornings, or something else? How about personal devotions? When children are able to read on their own, they can begin having daily time with God using age-appropriate devotional material. From pretty princesses to alpha males, there are bibles and devotionals on the market that target varying ages and interests. There is systematic character training material available from Character First!, a division of Strata and from the Institute of Basic Life Principles. Years ago, I was introduced to these companies and have been using their material ever since. There are also church-based groups like scouting and AWANA that support you in formally shaping character.

Informal character shaping gets plenty of opportunity to work its muscle in every-day living. I've found that maximizing on teachable moments is one of the best ways to cement a point. Teachable moments are everyday teachable opportunities born out of life events. Teachable moments take an on-the-spot occurrence and attach it to a biblical principle. An effective teachable moment begins with open communication between you and your child. Then, a catalyst or situation arises that calls for your attention. You then have an opportunity to address it with biblical truth. Recently, my daughter and I attended a school fair. We were speaking to a school representative about how to gain entry into their coveted program. Out of those that fit the criteria, there were still many applicants. When asked how they picked from those, she replied, "The squeaky wheel gets the oil". After we walked away, I took the time to explain to my daughter what that idiom meant. I told her that we would indeed be persistent in connecting with the school and that they'd get to know us by name. When we got to the car, I then had her turn to the Parable of the Judge and the Persistent Widow (Luke 18:1-8). This everyday moment turned into a teachable moment.

Storytelling is another great way to share character qualities. Some of my most fond childhood memories are of my dad telling me stories. And I'm not talking about as a little kid either. It was during my high school years that my dad told me the most stories. My husband and I both enjoy telling our children stories. Here is an example of a story on determination.

Frog in a Milk Pail[1]

A frog was hopping around a farmyard, when it decided to look around a barn. Suddenly overcome with thirst, he discovered a milk pail. The sight and smell of the milk were enticing so he jumped in. After a long drink, he discovered that he couldn't get out. He tried to stretch and kick his feet to push off the bottom of the pail but found it was too deep. There was too much milk in the bottom of the pail. He swam about trying to reach the top but the sides were too high. The frog kicked and thrashed about and kicked some more, determined not to give up. With the frog's churning about, the milk became butter. Solid enough to stand on, the frog stood in the butter and got out of the pail.

COACHING

Parenting and coaching are a lot alike. I have learned much from observing a great parent coach. Two of my children are on a competitive STEM team (as was mentioned earlier with my first born). Their coach, Mr. Randy is a true gem. Not only is he teaching them to be leaders in STEM but he is also building their character and "Training Them Up in The Way They Should Go" which is inscribed on their team shirts. I've watched this coach inspire, motivate, encourage and challenge the children in his program. I've watched him correct and redirect them. And I've watched him lead them to self-discovery. Under his tutelage, the children no longer say, "I don't know"; they say, "Let me find out how". As I've observed him, I've been taking notes and have adopted some of his strategies.

With my parent/coach hat on, I've tweaked my approach to shaping character. I invite you to try these strategies I've adopted from Mr. Randy. Instead of just telling your children what to do, involve them in the process. If decisions need to be made about their education, about their extra-curricular activities or even about a vacation, solicit their input. Instead of making accusations, pose open-ended questions to gain under-standing. As opposed to harping on everything they are doing wrong, focus on their strengths, abilities and potential. Shaping character is a never-ending process for both parent and child. But with Jesus at the helm, we are turning to look more and more like Him every day.

Being confident of this very thing, that He who has begun a good work in you will complete it until the day of Jesus Christ. Philippians 1:6

When your children's name comes up in conversation, it is your hope that they are spoken well of. As Martin Luther King, Jr. said, they "will be judged for the content of their character." How, then, will we help shape character worth commending? You've been in this book a few chapters now so you know what I'm going to say. It begins with…you know it, so say it…modeling. You have the distinct privilege of modeling before your children character befitting the Creator. Is your character imitable?

Have you ever played a game with young children where you imitate animals? Hop like a frog. Swing your trunk like an elephant. Act like a monkey. What about act like mommy? Be the daddy. What would that look like? Would you be proud of the reenactment?

Follow my example, as I follow the example of Christ. 1 Corinthians 11:1

When godly character is donned, it looks good on. When demonstrating their character, your children will stand out as beacons of light. Their peers will know them for being a friend to all. Elders will know them for being respectful. Their co-workers will know them for their availability. Your children will have thriving healthy relationships with God, family, friends, and the community. Why? Because of the content of their character. When their name is dropped, their character will precede them.

When we see their demonstrations of good character, let us be diligent in recognizing it. Just as swiftly as we address negative behavior, let us be even quicker in pointing out their godly character. Recently, during nightly family devotions, my son showed initiative in coming up with a game for the devotional. He created five questions and a bonus based on the verse we were studying. He threw a ball to the person who would answer the question. It was fun and engaging. I was very impressed with his initiative and creativity. I thanked him for showing initiative and creativity in coming up with the questions and I rewarded him with a pack of gum for this great idea.

Parents, it is a constant pouring in and a continuous investment of time, energy and effort. Every now and again though, you'd like to see a return on your investment, wouldn't you? Well, I'd venture to say your children are giving you a return. You just have to have eyes to see. Ask God to open your eyes to see the greatness in your children. And when you see what God sees, recognize them for it. We can be quick to catch a child committing an offense. Let's be even more quick to catch them doing good!

To be caught red-handed is to be caught with the evidence for all to see. Its origins date back to 15th century Scotland, where it was used when describing a criminal caught with the victim's blood on his hand. I have been known to catch my children red-handed. My natural inclination gravitates toward magnifying their errors then doling out corrective action. And perhaps that's just the nature of the beast for me with six young children. Pubescent kids, toddlers and a few in between, makes for a constant testing of the waters and feeling their way through while collecting life experience. And much of that experience comes about through trial and error. Remember, the home is a safe place for making mistakes.

God has gently whispered to me, what I'm going to whisper to you, "You've caught them red-handed; now catch them doing good!" At heart, I am an encourager. It's who I am. It's what I do. It's part of the reason you have this book in your hand, because I want to encourage you. I want you to know you CAN do this! I want you to know you are equipped for the task at hand. But I have to be intentional to ensure that same encouragement flows from my heart to my children. Don't you delight in seeing your children reach their potential? Do you like cheering them on at their games? But what happens when you've reminded, nudged, cajoled and motivated them to carry out the same chore day after day? Well, that encouragement takes on a new shape. Gone are the words of affirmation and here come the words of condemnation.

One autumn, my children and I attended an annual American Indian Festival. My then nine-year old Cub Scout in uniform was completing one of his electives on American Indian Life. While we were at the craft table, my son noticed several young girls find a phone on the ground. He got my attention and began telling me, "Mommy, these girls just found a phone on the ground". I lightly brushed it off, thinking he was just witnessing someone drop then pick up his or her own phone. He told me again, "No Mommy; that is not their phone. I heard them say "Ooh, look what I found." As he was relaying that information to me, the girls walked away with the phone. Then we heard a woman standing next to us say, "Where's my phone?" My son asked her if she lost her phone and she said yes. He said, "I saw the girls who took your phone." He then led the woman across the campgrounds to point out the girls so the woman could retrieve her phone. The woman was very grateful for his attentive eye and quick actions that led to her recovering her phone.

Here was a great example of an opportunity to catch him doing good and I almost missed it. I commended him on his attentiveness and shared the story with his extended family and Scout Den Leader. Love hopes the best and believes the best. So, even when what they are doing is contrary to what's expected, still hope for and believe the best about them. Instead of being so quick to highlight flaws, affirm the character you expect to see.

So, instead of telling your teen girl, "You're slacking on those dishes. I KNOW you see them in the sink. Why do I have to

ask you to do your job?" you could affirm her for the significant
role she plays since the kitchen is the central nervous system of
your home. When she completes the chore proactively you will
not say, "It's about time". You will acknowledge her for demonstrating responsibility.

> *Therefore encourage one another and build one another*
> *up, just as you are doing. 1 Thessalonians 5:11*

As we purposefully parent, let us be purposeful encouragers.
In Priscilla Shirer's book *The Resolution for Women*, she admonishes mothers to be intentional encouragers. Shirer states,
*"She [the mother] doesn't overlook their immaturity, mistakes and
mishaps; but when she brings these points up, there isn't a general air
of disapproval and low expectation. She chooses rather to temper her
honesty with the grace of edification and encouragement."* [10]

Remember this admonishment from the Apostle Paul;

> *Don't use foul or abusive language. Let everything you*
> *say be good and helpful, so that your words will be an*
> *encouragement to those who hear them. Ephesians 4:29.*

Let the words of our mouth minister love, hope and joy as
we purpose to catch them doing good. And for my grammarian
friends, I said it and I meant it…catch them doing GOOD. As
my Pastor would say, *"It ain't good English, but it's good preaching!"*

IN THE MIRROR

In all the character shaping being done in my house, what I'm finding is that the greatest shaping happening around here is my own. I'm learning to embrace acceptance, honor and humility, while laying to rest judgment and pride. I'm learning to truly love, seeing the best and believing the best about people. I'm learning to not only love others, but to love myself and to be gentle with myself. I'm learning to look in the mirror and affirm myself.

Not to exclude the men reading this book, but let me speak directly to the women for a moment. In her book, *Daring Greatly*, Brene Brown shares from her wealth of research that Motherhood is one of the greatest areas of shame, second only to a woman's looks. She asserts that we can combat this shame by exposing it, joining hands with others who are in the struggle and breaking free. She shares this simple yet powerful illustration. ... *"If we're at the grocery, and we push our cart past another mother whose child is screaming bloody murder and throwing Cheerios on the floor, we have a choice. If we choose to use the moment to confirm that we're better than she is, and that she's stuck in the web in ways we are not, we will roll our eyes in disapproval and walk by. Our other choice, though, is to flash that mother our best "you're not alone-I've been there, sister" smile because we know what she's feeling."*[11] Moms, can you relate? I've been right there with the tantrums. Who will join hands with me in a show of solidarity that we are not alone? Shame is not on us. Shame on the enemy for trying to trick us into thinking we are alone. Shame on him for trying to make us believe we live in silos. No, we join hands because I am my sister's keeper. My sister is me.

Parenting, with all its unpredictability is hard enough as it is. It's sad that well-meaning people in our circle add more shame to the mix. Your mother-in-law doesn't understand why you won't let them eat sugary breakfast cereals. Your mom doesn't understand why you won't let them watch TV. She says you watched TV and you turned out just fine. Your grandmother wants to know why you won't just spank him already.

And even if we are able to overcome that judgment, our own negative self-talk can get the best of us. In your mind, you can just hear perfect little mommy over there musing about why your kid has on his PJ's at the playground. Then another goes shaming herself for giving her kid Lunchables when crunchy mama over there in the Lululemon yoga pants walks by because you just know that her kid's got a bento box full of organic food.

Parents, let's vow to make parenting a judgment-free zone. A cousin was sharing with me some challenges she was having with her child. Out of her heart flowed love, frustration, exhaustion, and ambivalence about her relationship with her child. She said to me, "Please don't judge me." Far from judging, my mama heart hurt with her. Because I know from my own experiences how difficult it is to love your children. I know from experience that some days, hugs and kisses don't come easy. I know from experience that the work of parenting has developed my availability, my flexibility and my forgiveness. Yup; parenting has been one of the major character-shaping forces in my own life. How about you?

Aside from external judgment, we can be extremely critical of ourselves. Oh, the divide between the idealized version of the parent I long to be and the actual parent that I am. And as I look across that wide crevasse, I condemn mommy on this side for not looking and acting like the idealized mommy. The Apostle Paul said it so well.

> *For I have the desire to do what is good, but I cannot carry it out. For I do not do the good I want to do, but the evil I do not want to do—this I keep on doing.*
> *Romans 7:18b-19.*

You ever find yourself having a string of happy parenting days then you have one rough day and you're beating yourself up for being the worst parent ever? Do not fall for that trick of the enemy. Give thanks to God that He bridges the divide, He is the restorer of the breach, He is the one who teaches our children and ensures their peace. And while He's doing that for your children, He's doing it for you too. In the verses that follow Romans 7:19, Paul thanks God that through Jesus we are delivered! We are not held in the bondage of sin, of never measuring up and of self-condemnation.

Parenting is like a 20x lighted magnifying mirror. It exposes and brings into stark clarity every blackhead, whitehead, spot and blemish in our own character. But the beauty is God sees us not in our imperfection but through the cleansing blood of Jesus Christ.

In becoming a parent, you died to your old self. Parenting gave rise to a new you. A better you. Each day, parenting serves as a stimulus for shaping your character. Each day, you are compelled to be a better human being. Parenting is a spark that ignites you. It burns away the resin of selfishness and the sweet aroma of surrender goes up to God as an offering. He sees your surrender. He sees your sacrifice. He accepts your offering and pours you out a blessing you don't have room to receive. You are radically transformed. When you peer into the eyes of your precious baby, you are filled with unspeakable joy. When you stand and watch your child who has been diagnosed with too many conditions to list, graduate from high school you are overcome with gratitude. When you walk alongside another parent whose child has been exactly where yours has been, you are filled with compassion. Who knew parenting would be the vehicle God would use to revolutionize your life? As my grandmother used to say, "The Lord works in mysterious ways."

....

PRACTICAL APPLICATION

This week, recognize your child for their demonstration of godly character. Visit www.strataleadership.com to print a copy of character qualities. From the list, identify one character trait they've displayed recently. Tell your child what they did, name the specific trait and share the impact it had.

....

prayer

Lord, I thank you that I am your workmanship. It is under your skillful hand that my character is shaped. Thank you for shaping me in your image so that I can be an effective witness to my children. Father, come into my children's hearts and affirm for them that apart from you, they can do nothing. Reiterate for them the need to have a personal relationship with you. It is only through this relationship that they truly embrace and exemplify good godly character. Even though it is not always easy, I am grateful for the trials by fire that allow my children and me to look even more like you. As my children reflect your character, may they bring you glory and draw others closer to you.

~

Chapter 8

IN IT TO WIN IT

*For what will it profit a man if he gains the whole
world, and loses his own soul? Mark 8:36*

LET'S FACE IT; WE ARE all trying to raise children who will turn out to be productive adults. And secretly each of us wants our children to attain the American Dream. Be honest; when you visualize the future for your kids, do you see a hoopdy and an efficiency? Probably not. We all have goals for our children. They are the objectives that direct the choices we make in raising them. We all want our children to do "well" so they will be "successful" in life. We all beam with pride when our children get the honor roll, gain entry into the most exclusive schools, and make the cut on elite sports teams. We've come to accept these achievements as markers of success. With these childhood accomplishments, we may feel that they are on their way to living the good life. The question we must ask is do we want them to live a "good" life or a godly life?

Inasmuch as we want them to do well, we've been charged with a mission far greater. Our role is not simply to help them acquire more things. Our role is not to manufacture the next compliant worker of a Fortune 500 company. With the end in mind parents, we've got to keep our focus on what's truly at stake. What hangs in the balance is where our children will spend eternity. Looking back at the foundational scripture for this chapter, what good will it really do for our children if they acquire every worldly good but lose their souls? And we see this illustrated in life. When lottery winners come into huge sums of cash, more than half of them end up broke. When people nearing the end of life are asked what they would have done differently, many answer they would not have worked so hard and would have put more energy into relationships and fulfilling their dreams.

"Instruct those who are rich in this present world not to be conceited or to fix their hope on the uncertainty of riches, but on God, who richly supplies us with all things to enjoy. Instruct them to do good, to be rich in good works, to be generous and ready to share, storing up for themselves the treasure of a good foundation for the future, so that they may take hold of that which is life indeed" (1 Timothy 6:17-19).

Let's get to the heart of it. We all want our children to do well. And we would all love to see a return on our investment. It's why we take them to piano class, gymnastics, and chess practice all in the same week. While extracurricular activities are good, what is the ultimate goal you wish to achieve in raising your children? Is your end goal to raise a well-rounded individual? Is your goal to raise a kid with an extensive resume?

Has most of your parenting centered on raising children who "look good"? Do we want to raise children who will just do good and be good? Good children will be by-products of raising godly children. When reared in the admonition of the Lord, they will be good and they will do good. The word says every good and perfect gift is from above. It also says children are a gift. Your children are a good and perfect gift from the Lord to this world. And when they are rooted in the things of Christ, they will bear good fruit.

With the all-consuming nature of our secular society, it is easy to leave God out of our child rearing. The lust of the flesh, the lust of the eyes and the pride of life are thorns that have grown to choke out the need for God in the lives of our children. Well-meaning beliefs, attitudes, events and activities have edged God closer to the periphery of our children's lives and at times it's been the parent's own hand nudging God away. We don't want to be found guilty of having taught them to lie by saying we aren't home when we really are. We don't want to be the one's having taught them to steal by taking supplies from our jobs. We don't want to be the one forsaking having taught them the word because we are so busy with their extracurricular activities. Jesus says it would be better for a millstone to be around our necks than to lead His children astray (Luke 17:1-2). The world is vying for their attention; let us not further contribute to that with an overemphasis on worldly things.

With the end in mind, we should be more concerned about our children's salvation than offering momentary pleasure. My most immediate concern as their parent is not about their happiness. I don't want to lose you here so please hear me out. I want my children to be filled with love, joy, and laughter. But my focus in rearing them does not center on their happiness. It is a delight to offer them fun and enriching life experiences. It is also a bane to them, I'm sure, to have parents that expect them to live up to their full potential. Because reaching that potential requires work and truth be told, children aren't always eager to work. Can somebody with a phlegmatic teenage boy give me a high five?

Building character is not easy work and children will not always feel up to the challenge. That is why it requires fastidious parents with the end in mind consistently reminding them of who they are in God. The appeal to be lazy, to be a follower and to regurgitate what's happening in the culture is strong. The current takes those swept up in the culture of the day. If we are not careful, our children will be swept away by those raging rapids. Living a godly life forces them to swim upstream. Moving counter culture is not easy and requires holy strength. They may not be running to the front of the line for scripture memorization, church several days a week or reading books as opposed to watching TV. But that conditioning fortifies them to choose God over things of this world.

If your dad was anything like mine, every day wasn't a happy day at home. Did I want to have history lessons at home? No! Did I want to complete at home book reports? No! As a teen, I didn't understand why I couldn't stay up until 11pm so I could watch The Arsenio Hall Show. I guess I'm telling my age there. "What do you mean I can't go to the party?!" "Why can't I wear a miniskirt?" I'd venture to say, my happiness at that moment wasn't his primary concern. His concern was to love me enough to protect me from foolishness. His concern was to help me become a great thinker. His concern was to help me discover my gifts and use them appropriately.

RAISING TODAY'S CHILDREN

It's not easy being a parent these days. The financial strain causes most families to have both parents working outside the home. And single parents, my heart goes out to you as you trust the Holy Spirit and rely on Him to assist you in raising your children. I pray an abundance of grace for my blended families that are doing their best to seamlessly merge together. And where is the village they say is needed to raise children? The villagers seem to have scattered—the village of grandparents, aunts, uncles, older cousins and neighbors. In raising our families, we face direct opposition from a culture that says children are a burden, not a blessing. It is a culture that even esteems pets above children. Children interfere with your ability to have a "good" life; that's what the world pushes on us.

It's not easy being a kid these days either. They've got it even harder. Social media usage is a daily way of life. Kids are constantly plugged in and we know what we consume is who we become. "Facebook Depression", cyber bullying, and sexting are causing increases in anxiety and lowering self-esteem. The selfie phenomenon has caused our children to become narcissistic and the types of selfies they are taking can lead to increased sexual promiscuity. Parents, our world is in crisis. Yet, much of our thinking and doing with and for our children is on superficial things. We are concerned about our children "doing good", "looking good" and "being good". And those are all fine and good but only as long as they occur within the context of building Christian character. And their character muscle will have to be strong to contend with what they are facing. We are in a war for their souls (1 Peter 2:11).

COUNTER CULTURE

Our children are in the world but not of it. As a result, we must protect them from being sidetracked by worldly pursuits. We must protect them from the lure of worldly living. Remember Eve? She was seduced by the lure of worldly grandiose thinking. Just as the prince of this world deceived Eve, he will use the same tactics on us and on our children. Do we want to give him an open door into our homes and let him stay in our guest room? We run the risk of doing that by chasing worldly pursuits.

We can fall right into that snare in our pursuits of doing good, looking good and being good for the sake of appearances.

> *"I have given them your word and the world has hated them, for they are not of the world any more than I am of the world. My prayer is not that you take them out of the world but that you protect them from the evil one. They are not of the world, even as I am not of it."*
> *John 17:14-16*

It is mission critical that our children are in it to win it. Not only are they fighting against the grain to boldly proclaim Christ for themselves, they have to operate within a culture that is currently turning away from the Gospel at a rapid pace. They have to be rooted in what they believe as to not only stand in their convictions but also to draw others into the kingdom. The state of the Church is in crisis. As mentioned earlier, many that were raised in church are turning away from the faith. I can only imagine the effects on the subsequent generation. Hence, the time is NOW to affect change. Our children will be instrumental in reversing the tide and this is a big ship to turn so it's going to take an army. Are your children ready to enlist? While our children must operate within the context of secular society, they are to stand up and stand out for God. "But you are a chosen people, a royal priesthood, a holy nation, God's special possession, that you may declare the praises of him who called you out of darkness into his wonderful light." 1 Peter 2:9

When polled, many Americans identify as Christian but very few of those actually practice their faith.[12] We want our children to live their faith out loud. We want them to not merely live a shadow of our faith, but we want them to pursue healthy, thriving relationships with the Father. Not just in word, but also in their hearts and in the actions, our prayer should be that our children live lives totally surrendered to Christ. They will witness from our own behavior that life is not about the acquisition of things or being forever busy, but instead about loving, giving and serving. Because here's what the world is dishing out and it's in stark contrast to how God would have us to live.

Godly	Worldly
Raised by the Word	Raised as a Friend
Fruit of the Spirit	Personal Happiness
Godly Character	Self Centered, Me Culture
Respect for Authority	Rejection of Authority
Purity	Oversexualization
Childlike Wonder, Hope	Cynicism
Contentment	Indulgent, Excess
Obedience	Disobedient, Rebellious
Respectful, Humble	Aggressive, Arrogant
Absolute Truth	Post Modernism
Surrender	Control
Submission	Power Struggle
Holiness	Acceptance of Sin

Just how are these worldly invasions presented to us? Sometimes they come packaged quite innocently and can be deceiving if we aren't paying close attention. Parents, we have to pray for eyes to see and ears to hear because if we aren't careful we can miss it. But rest assured your children won't miss it. Have you watched TV with your children lately? In the last 20 years, we've seen the construct of family completely rewritten on TV. Excessive violence, sexual immorality, and instant gratification through the acquisition of things seem to be the order of the day. Today's top-rated programs show lead characters praised for sexual immorality and murder. You can't even safely watch a cooking show with your child because there are curse words aplenty and nakedness in the commercials.

Who doesn't like going to the movies, resting in a comfy, oversized leather recliner and munching on popcorn? Geez, it would be great if we could do that and watch a wholesome movie devoid of lewd and crude humor. Has the G-rated movie completely disappeared? One of the biggest movie producers is known for planting hidden sexual messaging in their films and as mentioned earlier demonizes the role of mother. And what about music? All you have to do is turn on the current pop station and you'll get an earful.

It doesn't end there. Messaging on children's clothing and clothing that is inappropriate for the age is the trend. Introduction to the occult, dark arts and vampirism through TV shows, books and movies is commonplace. Posters and billboards continuously inviting the eye to feast on fast food and liquor are seen daily. Parents, my heart is so grieved. Our children are under constant attack. We must not just take a defensive stance but rather offensively thwart the assault. But that's difficult when the enemy has been so crafty to have us so consumed that we can't even eat a meal together at the table because we are moving in a hundred different directions at dinnertime. Though the attack is pervasive, we will stand firm in our convictions.

> *"But if serving the Lord seems undesirable to you, then choose for yourselves this day whom you will serve, whether the gods your ancestors served beyond the Euphrates, or the gods of the Amorites, in whose land you are living. But as for me and my household, we will serve the Lord." Joshua 24:15*

THE RESULT

After Joshua led the Israelites, God's chosen people, into the promised land they served the Lord throughout Joshua's lifetime. After Joshua and those of his generation died, the next generation grew up and did not know the Lord nor did they know what He had done for Israel. They did what was evil in the sight of the Lord (Judges 2). You can pause here to go read Judges Chapter 2.

How is it that a people who were favored by God and who inherited a great blessing move so far away from God in one generation? How is it that they did not know the Lord? How is it that they did not know what the Lord had done for their parents? Think about this carefully. Where was the disconnect?

I reckon it had to lie with the parents. This is tough, I know. Parents let US not be the reason a whole generation knows nothing of the Lord.

In our pursuit of living successful lives, let us be mindful not to leave God out of the equation. The acquisition of a big house, nice cars, and degrees can choke out our drive for God. While God has said He wants us to have life and have it more abundantly and while God desires to bless us, He certainly does not intend for that to come at the expense of having a healthy, thriving relationship with Him. Our children should witness in us a greater hunger and zeal for Christ than for things. Let us not be the catalyst for future generations moving farther away from the Gospel.

How then do we avoid this generational departure? Parents, we must pass on the fear of the LORD to our children and our children's children. We must do everything we can to leave a legacy and passion for living the Truth in accordance with God's commands. Our walk with God will speak volumes. Let us not be hypocrites. We must be diligent in instructing them in His ways. If we live compromised lives, we pass on a legacy of compromise. This is how we can end up with a generation that calls themselves Christian in name but not in everyday lifestyle. It is then false religion and not relationship that is perpetuated. Oh, the heartbreak at the thought of the next generation living a form of godliness that is devoid of the power and presence of God. If we don't address this with full fervor and immediacy, the results will be dire.

THERE IS HOPE

Parents, there is hope. For those already on their knees, in it to win it, I commend you. Let us all be reminded,

> *"If my people, who are called by my name, will humble themselves and pray and seek my face and turn from their wicked ways, then I will hear from heaven, and I will forgive their sin and will heal their land."*
> *2 Chronicles 7:14*

We must get on our faces and repent. We must commit to leading by example. We must put on our armor and stand. We must mark our territory. We must anoint our children. Our homes are holy ground. As Paul instructed Timothy, admonish your children to carefully guard the good deposit that was placed into their care (2 Timothy 1:14). Remind your children to not be conformed to the patterns and behaviors of this world but to renew their minds (Romans 12:1-2).

In addition to living out our Christian values before our children, we have to protect them. Remember Mary and Joseph fled to Egypt to hide Jesus from Herod. Our homes are to be a refuge. Our homes shall be their safe haven where the evil one has no foothold. Our homes are to be inoculated from the poison of the world. Just as some receive vaccinations to prevent the contraction of contagious disease, the blood of Jesus vaccinates our hearts and homes. The godly home is a safe haven from the oppression of worldly lifestyles. In the safety of your home, your 12-year old can still play with dolls if she wants to without ridicule. In the sanctity of your home, your children can be themselves.

Not too far from my home is a wildlife sanctuary for Canadian Geese. A conservationist who gave much of his life in service to protecting wildlife established the sanctuary. His sanctuary was a place where thousands of geese came to feed and rest. Isn't that much like your home? Safe from the wiles of the world, your home is a safe haven, a respite place for your children or for anyone for that matter who needs a place of safety.

Parents, God trusts you so much He placed His little flock in your care. He's counting on you to direct their hearts to Him. He expects you to be in it to win it for the kingdom. But first, He wants to sit with you and ask you some questions. Come closer.

So, when they had eaten breakfast, Jesus said to Simon Peter, "Simon, son of Jonah, do you love Me more than these?" He said to Him, "Yes, Lord; You know that I love You." He said to him, "Feed My lambs." He said to him again a second time, "Simon, son of Jonah, do you love Me?" He said to Him, "Yes, Lord; You know that I love You." He said to him, "Tend My sheep." He said to him the third time, "Simon, son of Jonah, do you love Me?" Peter was grieved because He said to him the third time, "Do you love Me?" And he said to Him, "Lord, You know all things; You know that I love You." Jesus said to him, "Feed My sheep." John 21:15-17

Parents, like Peter, God has placed you in a position of authority and influence. Like Peter, God is entrusting to you the responsibility of helping establish His church. Your children are the church. Remember, Jesus tells us that the kingdom of heaven belongs to them. We need to take note. Take a page from what Jesus says. They are kingdom advancers. They are kingdom keepers. They are kingdom kids.

Parents, Jesus wants to know if you love Him enough to set aside your plans, your agenda, your time, your resources, and your many skills to love Him and to love what's important to Him. Jesus identifies the ways that you can demonstrate your love for Him. Remember, love denotes action and He implores you to live out your love for Him. And just how can you do that? You can show your love for the Master by feeding His lambs. Your children are His lambs. They are not yet mature and are vulnerable. They need direction and guidance. They need to be held close to your bosom. He calls for you to tend His sheep. To tend His sheep is to train them up in the way they should go. He desires for you to feed His sheep. He longs for you to gradually begin them on solids. Just as your newborn baby can only handle milk, your young children have to be fed and engaged in the things of God in a way they can understand. As your children mature and the worldly assaults become even more pervasive, you will have to keep pace. You not only want them to know what you believe, but you want to be able to make a compelling case for Christ. You want to be able to articulate *why* you believe what you believe.

It is a great responsibility to shepherd His precious little ones. Careful nurturing calls for us to keep them safe and held close to the Father. Lambs and sheep without careful feeding and tending are doomed. They are led astray, killed by predators or die of starvation. Have you ever witnessed any children you know or have heard about children that were not carefully tended? What became of them? Jehovah-Raah, The Lord My Shepherd dutifully leads, guides and protects us and He expects us to do likewise with the little flock He's entrusted into our care. And might I stick a pin here as a reminder that Jesus refers to the children as HIS lambs and HIS sheep. Be reminded that your children do not belong to you. You are merely tending the flock. They belong to Jesus.

And what about the wayward one? In all our diligence, there will still be the one that goes astray. Keep the faith parents. Don't lose hope. There is a great promise even for the wayward one. Jehovah-Raah will leave the 99 to go after your ONE. *"What do you think? If a man owns a hundred sheep, and one of them wanders away, will he not leave the ninety-nine on the hills and go to look for the one that wandered off. And if he finds it, truly I tell you, he is happier about that one sheep than about the ninety-nine that did not wander off. In the same way your Father in heaven is not willing that any of these little ones should perish."* Matthew 18:12-14 That is great news worth shouting about!

RESOLVE

Seeing the magnitude of what we're facing, resolve to move forward with persistence. Be diligent in redeeming the time, as the days are evil (Ephesians 5:16). Do not allow the cares of this world to choke out your time with your children. They are growing by the second and if you blink too long, precious moments will pass you by. Learn how to embrace the now moment and teach your children to do the same. Help your children train their eyes and ears to experience God in the now moment. Skip rocks together, plant a garden, watch a bird soar, and listen to cicadas buzz. Teach your children to be still and know that He is God and He is here.

We have to set our intentions on raising the next generation of Daniels. We will encourage our children to be courageous in the face of fear knowing God will never leave nor forsake them. By teaching them who they are in Christ, we enable them to take a stand even when it it's unpopular. My children have certainly had a taste of this in bringing vegetarian lunches to school everyday. We have to help them know that no temptation has to overtake them because God has made a way of escape (1 Corinthians 10:13). Just like Daniel was able to stand as the sizzling platters of meat went past him, our children will be able to withstand temptation.

When our children take a stand for righteousness' sake, God will see their efforts and reward them handsomely. Just as God saw Nehemiah's desire to rebuild the wall and blessed him with provision, God will see your children's efforts and will bless them accordingly. Your children will be elevated to positions of authority and influence like Joseph and Deborah so that they help others. Your children will have discernment like Joshua and the Shunamite Woman, sensing when God is near. They will be able to rightly divide lies from truth. They will be wise to the wiles of Satan and not be ensnared in sin traps. And in the face of near constant distractions, they will have their face set about their Father's business. They are in it to win it. Actively pursuing Christ, sharing the Good News and helping those who need the most help, yes, they are in the world but not of it. They are indeed in it to win it.

PRACTICAL APPLICATION

Based on your child's age, watch a secular show or listen to a current pop song. Discuss the theme of the show or song. Highlight how it conflicts with the Truth of God's word.

Also, consider the amount of time your children spend on electronic devices, television and extracurricular activities. Consider how much time they spend on activities that build faith and Christian character. Based on where their time is being spent, are they sufficiently being armed to be in it to win it? Will you need to make modifications? Pray and ask for wisdom on how to best use your time, effort and resources to shape godly versus worldly children.

prayer

God, my heart is heavy. I first come to say I'm sorry. Lord, I repent for the ways I've played right into the hand of the enemy and allowed myself to be distracted and detracted from teaching my children Your will and Your way. There have been times I've permitted seemingly good things to edge you out. Lord, guide my steps as I strive to keep You at the center. Let me be diligent in not only wanting my children to be good but more than that let me be diligent in consistently pointing their hearts back to you. Lord, help me make my home a safe haven for your children. Lord, let me be persistent in protecting them, guiding them and feeding them so that they are duly equipped to withstand. And when it is time for them to win others, through your guidance, they will be duly equipped for the task. Thank you for protecting them from the evil one as they go about Your business of sharing the Good News throughout the earth.

Chapter 9

GROWING WISE STANDING TALL

And Jesus grew in wisdom and stature, and
in favor with God and man. Luke 2:52

AT SOME POINT, WE'VE ALL said, prayed, hoped or thought I want my children to be better off than me. That's part of why we work so hard to provide the best life, right? How then do we qualify being better off? Living in a bigger house? More education? To not struggle as much? To not have to work as hard? To not have to hurt so deeply? In what ways do we really want our children to be better off than us? I would speculate most of us want them to live truly fulfilled lives.

Yes, you want the absolute best for your children. I do too. But when I strip it down to the bare bones, outside of having a thriving relationship with God, I want them to have love in their hearts and to be wise. The bible tells us wisdom is the principal thing. Wisdom is the key that unlocks the door to the fulfilled life. And in order to train them in growing wise, we parents need wisdom. We can't effectively raise children today without it. None of us come into the job of parenting knowing exactly what to do. While we may know how to meet their temporal needs, it takes wisdom from on high to nurture budding hearts. Fortunately, God says if we ask for wisdom, He'll dole it out liberally. *If any of you lacks wisdom, you should ask God, who gives generously to all without finding fault, and it will be given to you. James 1:5*

Wisdom is not merely smarts. Wisdom is not intellect. Wisdom is not knowledge. Wisdom takes all the preceding into account and uses sound judgment to take the best course of action. God gave me a simple two-word phrase that sums up wisdom. As I was sitting in a retreat waiting for my turn as the next speaker, God said, "You will not be using your prepared notes. Put them away." Panic swept over me. Lord, what do you mean I'm not going to use my notes? I prepared long and hard for this moment. How I am going to close out this life-changing three-day event? I am already coming behind a dynamic speaker and am feeling inadequate and you want me to toss these notes? What am I supposed to say? What am I supposed to do? My thoughts were running rampant. I reached over to my friend and told her, "There's no need for me to speak. The person speaking is doing so well we can just let her close it out." She sweetly told me, "No. You're still going to speak." I went to the bathroom to try to collect myself.

This was very new territory for me. While I am a speaker, I never do a talk on the fly. I always have talking points. I like to succinctly hit my points and keep the talk focused. Well, here I stood in the bathroom with nothing. No ideas, No notes. No confidence. Nothing. Nothing that is but Jesus. I looked in the mirror and said God tell me what to say. He simply replied, *"Deuteronomy 30:19."* *"This day I call the heavens and the earth as witnesses against you that I have set before you life and death, bless-ings and curses. Now choose life, so that you and your children may live."* He said, *"Tell my people to choose well."* Yup, that was all He said, CHOOSE WELL. With that, I gathered myself, went back into the room and told the people what He said.

That nugget of wisdom has been ringing true since that day two years ago. He continues to tell me to admonish the people to choose well. And that's what wisdom does. It takes what you know and compels you to choose well. Wisdom gives insight so you are equipped to choose well. Wisdom gives you the courage to do the right thing so you can choose well. Wisdom gives you the discernment to properly assess a situation so you can choose well.

Regardless of what we do, the clock is ticking and our chil-dren are growing. Prayerfully, we will be wise and circumspect, following exactly what God tells us to do regarding our chil-dren. In carefully heeding His voice, we will choose well in our parenting. As our children grow and mature, it is our hope that they will choose well. Remember in the last chapter when we said our children are in the world, not of it? They will grow up right alongside the tares (Matthew 13:36-43). The tares represent people and situations with the appearance of good but are not the genuine article. Wisdom will be the tool that separates wheat from tares. Wisdom will allow your children to choose well when it comes to whom to befriend, what college to attend, and what job to take.

Continual growth, including growing wise, is a hallmark of the Believer. *"Being confident of this, that he who began a good work in you will carry it on to completion until the day of Christ Jesus. Philippians 1:6* It is a lifelong process that even Jesus himself went through. Even though He is God incarnate, He walked through the maturation process so that we can learn from it. Jesus' growth from humanity to divinity was an arduous task filled with many tests and trials, yet, He walked it out beautifully. And all along the way, His Father kept him, covered Him, encouraged Him, provided for Him, and gave Him earthly support.

Using the Father's model, let us undergird our children for the journey.

Kept—Remember when Joseph and Mary fled to protect their son from Herod's wrath? Several times, the Pharisees were ready to have Jesus stoned, yet, He escaped unharmed. How are you keeping your children covered?

Encouraged—The Father spoke words of affirmation over Jesus; this is my beloved Son in whom I am well pleased (Matthew 3:17). How often do your children hear you speaking well of them?

Provided—Spiritual provision was granted during Jesus' 40 days & nights in the wilderness. Under the strain of laborious travel during His earthly ministry, Jesus was cared for. What types of provision are you offering your children outside of immediate food, clothing and shelter?

Supported—The disciples and friends of Jesus loved, cared for, and supported Him and His ministry. Apart from yourself, what support systems have you put in place for your children?

GROWING IN WISDOM

Growth also requires a firm foundation. Trees can grow taller when connected to a thriving root system. Think about the root system that is supporting your children's growth. A part of their root system is their village. When Jesus dispatched the 70, He sent them out two by two. Paul told Timothy to take what he had been taught and teach it to others. Mutual support is necessary as iron sharpens iron. Who is the "iron" in your child's life? Who is in your child's village?

Given the current climate of post modernism, atheism and defection from the Church, our children need to be duly equipped to grow in their faith. For this reason, they must have a sound understanding of what we believe and why we believe it. That means that we parents must fully grasp the basic tenets of Christianity. We must *know* what we believe so we can impart this truth to our children. Accepting Christ as Lord and personal Savior is not just an emotional experience. A living faith is not merely thinking or feeling but knowing. And Christian growth integrates spirituality, theology, and ethics in conjunction with faith for the basis of belief.

> *But in your hearts revere Christ as Lord. Always be prepared to give an answer to everyone who asks you to give the reason for the hope that you have. But do this with gentleness and respect. 1 Peter 3:15*

Your children's ability to grow in wisdom and in stature is limitless. Given the right conditions, they will be positioned to prosper. In the loving, capable, secure arms of a nurturing parent, children have the opportunity to blossom to their full potential. Jesus was the son of a carpenter. He grew up in an everyday working class family. In His humanity, He grew in wisdom and stature. In fact, He was so astute, that as a child He sat reasoning in the temple courts. The adults with Him were amazed by His level of understanding and answers (Luke 2:46-47). Do you give your children an opportunity to engage in open dialogue with adults or are they relegated to "a child's place"?

A liberal dispensation of wisdom happens when we meet God in prayer. He longs to teach us and to teach our children but do we slow down enough to listen? Is our prayer time filled with requests alone? In addition to prayer, wisdom is gained under the tutelage of the council (Proverbs 19:20-21, Job 12:12-13). Going back to the village, who is in your child's village dispensing wise counsel? When your child is a good listener and has a teachable spirit, they will grow wise.

The child who grows in wisdom possesses the key to living the blessed life. Take heed to these words from Solomon. *Blessed are those who find wisdom, those who gain understanding, for she is more profitable than silver and yields better returns than gold. She is more precious than rubies; nothing you desire can compare with her. Long life is in her right hand; in her left hand are riches and honor. Her ways are pleasant ways, and all her paths are peace. She is a tree of life to those who take hold of her; those who hold her fast will be blessed. By wisdom the Lord laid the earth's foundations, by understanding he set the heavens in place; by his knowledge the watery depths were divided, and the clouds let drop the dew. My son, do not let wisdom and understanding out of your sight, preserve sound judgment and discretion; they will be life for you, an ornament to grace your neck. Then you will go on your way in safety, and your foot will not stumble. When you lie down, you will not be afraid; when you lie down, your sleep will be sweet. Have no fear of sudden disaster or of the ruin that overtakes the wicked, for the Lord will be at your side and will keep your foot from being snared. Proverbs 3:13-26*

GROWING IN STATURE

To grow in stature is to advance both physically and spiritually. In the Old Testament, stature was primarily used to describe physical qualities while in the New Testament it was used as a measure of wisdom, maturity and righteousness in addition to referring to physical characteristics. Let us examine both of these in greater detail.

188 → PURPOSEFUL PARENTING

PHYSICAL GROWTH

We can deduce that Jesus was physically strong as he travelled extensively in His youth and during His years in ministry. When Jesus made the trek from Nazareth to Jerusalem for Passover, it is estimated that He would have travelled nearly 120 miles. We can venture to say He would have been pretty fit to journey from Galilee to Jerusalem and back, from Capernaum to Cana and Nazareth and back. Some estimate that Jesus travelled over 20,000 miles throughout his lifetime.[13]

If the body is to be used as an instrument of service (Romans 12:1, 6:12-13) and is the temple of the Holy Spirit (1 Corinthians 6:19-20) it should be handled with care. I've heard it said that we ought to pass on generational wealth to our children. To that I say yes. But I think it's equally important to pass along a generational blessing of health. Eating right, exercise, rest, proper hygiene and purity are all ways we should encourage our children to grow in stature. In this way, they are presenting their bodies holy and acceptable to God (Romans 12:1). What intentional steps are you taking to ensure your children are honoring their temples?

I would be remiss if I didn't talk about this further. We want to train our children to be obedient to Christ but that includes what they do to their bodies. Most parents I see ensure their children practice good hygiene. Many parents I know have demonstrated great courage in proactively teaching their children about sex, relationships and purity. But I see a void when it comes to teaching children about honoring their bodies through proper nourishment, rest and exercise. With the frenetic pace many families engage in today, little time is dedicated to cooking healthy meals, resting the body and exercising regularly. But I'm encouraging you as the Lord has encouraged me; do not grieve the spirit by what you and your children are consuming. I implore you to choose well and to train your children to do the same.

"He's a picky eater. Oh, she'll never eat that. He doesn't eat anything green." I've heard parents say it all regarding their children's food habits. I am persuaded that children can and will eat healthy foods. The onus is on the parent to know the way, go the way then show the way. The home is a ministry center for nourishing the spirit, the mind and the body. Just as we train them up to respect authority, to do well in school, and do their best in their extracurricular activities, we have to train them to care for their health by consuming foods that nourish and honor the temple. *Train up a child in the way he should go, And when he is old he will not depart from it. Proverbs 22:6*

Training children to desire nourishing food can actually begin in the uterus. Flavors are actually transmitted through amniotic fluid. Flavors are also present in breast milk. So, early on we can introduce our children to a wide variety of flavors. We can acclimate them to the tastes from different cultures; from a luscious curry to a crisp stir-fry, let them sample it all. That goes for you too. What new dishes have you tried lately? It all goes back to modeling, remember?

My heart is torn when I see parents adopt new eating habits, yet, let their children continue to consume unhealthy foods on a consistent basis. Perhaps parents are thinking, "My child just won't eat healthy. They'll never try any weird food. I just want peace; I don't want to fight." I know it's hard Mom and Dad, but we've got to be creative, diligent, persistent and insistent on helping our children eat right. My favorite meal as a kid was Kraft macaroni and cheese with fried chicken wings and canned corn. My mother, bless her heart, did the best she could. She was the baby girl in her family and never really learned to cook. But when we know better, God holds us accountable to do better. And with today's mass education of eating local, shopping farmer's markets and joining Community Supported Agriculture (CSA) Farms, the exposure is there. So, connect with your kids in the kitchen.

For those that desire a better way, God will honor the desires of your heart. He can and will redeem the time and restore the years that have already passed. Do you desire to change your family's eating habits but don't know how to get them on board? Try these tips.

- Let them help create the menu
- Invite them in the kitchen when you are preparing meals
- Let them choose one new item each week from the grocery store.
- Take them to places that are rich in new food experiences ("Taste of" events, food festivals)
- Serve food in the "make your own plate" style. This works well for Taco Bar, Baked Potato Bar, Stir-Fry Bowls

- Teach them what a serving size looks like
- Start by making simple swaps (white rice out, quinoa in)
- Teach them to read food labels

A McDonald's coupon booklet came in the mail and my daughter wanted the fries. I told her to look up the ingredients. Once she saw the list, she said never mind. Another time, she got a rice krispie treat from a school party. I told her to read the list of ingredients. She came across a few items that she couldn't pronounce, including tert-Butylhydroquinone (TBHQ). This additive, found in many packaged foods, is a preservative and in high doses is a carcinogenic. In addition to food, it is used industrially as a stabilizer to inhibit corrosion and is added to varnishes and lacquers. Needless to say, we got a good laugh out of that one. She went on to eat the treat but hasn't eaten one ever again. "TBHQ" and "High Fructose Corn Syrup" are now running jokes over here. Every time my children see something unhealthy like a Poptart everyone yells, "High Fructose Corn Syrup". Even my eight-year old reads the labels and if she sees sugar listed in the first five ingredients she'll tell her siblings, "That's not healthy!"

I know change is possible. The children of a friend would only eat pancakes for breakfast and chicken nuggets or fish sticks for dinner. That was their norm for several years. As God began to reveal a better plan to my friend, she slowly adopted new healthy habits. It has since become a family affair. And that is my prayer for all families. Studies predict that for the first time in history, the next generation is poised to have a shorter life span than their parents. And what makes that even more tragic is that the decline in life expectancy is primarily due to obesity-related diseases that are largely preventable.

When trying new things, they may not be adopted right away. One of my children never liked oatmeal. But every time we had oatmeal I requested she take two courtesy bites. Guess who loves oatmeal now? It took her until she was nine to develop a liking for it but now she loves it. And this morning, we had oatmeal and she was the first one happily lapping it up. Studies suggest it takes eight to ten tries of something that one says they do not like before it's adopted. So, encourage your child to take their two courtesy bites. Before you know it, they'll have a broad pallet.

My two oldest children are at the age where they are making some of their own food choices. At home, they are presented with healthy foods. When at a friend's house, church event, family function or school, they know I trust them to choose well. The lure of sugary treats, sodas and high fat foods can be very tempting. But they've been duly equipped to make the choice that will honor their temples. Occasionally, they'll indulge and that's okay too. We try to follow the 80/20 rule. 80% of the time we eat unprocessed, healthy whole food. The other 20% we give ourselves flexibility to eat an ice cream cone on the weekend or have pizza.

Change is a process. I know it would be a lot easier to grab a boxed starch already seasoned, take a protein and douse it in a ready-made sauce, heat some canned veggies and call everyone to the table for dinner. I've got six kids, so I get it. I know it's easier to go through the drive through on the nights you have extracurricular activities. But do your best to commit to eating REAL food and take it one step at a time. Call a family meeting and explain why you're making these changes. Adopt some of the tips above. While it may be tough, just like anything else with parenting, you make the tough decision out of your love for your children. And you love them enough to say I won't let you eat junk masquerading as food. Remember, no passive parenting.

The Lord gave me a major revelation as related to the health of my children and their children to come. I was filling out some initial new patient forms, one of which was the family history. I went down the line checking off ailment after ailment that my mother, grandmother and other immediate family members have suffered. Diabetes, high blood pressure, cancer, glaucoma, migraines, autoimmune disorders and more...check, check, check. In that moment, the Lord said, "The choices you make today will break the curse". In church, we talk about breaking generational curses and the Lord was telling me how I could have a direct impact on breaking some of the health curses over my family. He said, "Choose well and your children won't have to check some of these boxes and then their children will check even fewer." Praise God for revelation, for teaching me how to nourish my family and for enabling me to carry it out. And since He is no respecter of persons, He can do the same for you.

So, out of my love for my children even if they don't always like it, I'm training them to choose well when it comes to food. Sure, they'd probably like some McDonald's fries on a Friday night but when I think about the 17 ingredients in there…I just can't. My goodness, shouldn't it just be potatoes, salt and oil? And sure, I feel for them when they are ostracized at school for having "weird" food. Whenever your children feel ostracized, it just provides another great opportunity to remind them of what God says about them. And he says they are a peculiar people, a chosen generation, and a royal priesthood (1 Peter 2:9).

The food you offer your children each day is making an impression not only on their taste buds in the moment but is being coded in their brains. They are developing a preference for salt, fat and sugar. It is my prayer that they would desire foods that nourish and honor their bodies. In addition to fueling their bodies, encourage them to step away from the screens and get their bodies moving. Dance, play basketball, ride your scooter, ride your bike, roller skate, hoola hoop, do something to get that body moving. Then wrap it up with a good night's rest. Even teenagers need an early bedtime (they won't like me for saying so but it's true). Let us remain diligent in training our children to honor their temples.

SPIRITUAL GROWTH

For our children to grow in stature spiritually means to look more like Jesus every day. As they draw nearer to him, adopting the mind of Christ, they will mature and grow wise.

We can model for them the practice of growing in spiritual stature by daily abiding in God's presence, prayer, the study of His word, and serving others. Just as we discipline the physical body, we strengthen and train our spiritual muscle as well. What a delight it is for a parent to see their child coming into the fullness of Christ for themselves. *And He Himself gave some to be apostles, some prophets, some evangelists, and some pastors and teachers, for the equipping of the saints for the work of ministry, for the edifying of the body of Christ, till we all come to the unity of the faith and of the knowledge of the Son of God, to a perfect man, to the measure of the stature of the fullness of Christ; that we should no longer be children, tossed to and fro and carried about with every wind of doctrine, by the trickery of men, in the cunning craftiness of deceitful plotting, but, speaking the truth in love, may grow up in all things into Him who is the head—Christ—Ephesians 4:11-15*

FAVOR WITH GOD

Have you ever heard children talk about who's the favorite? Maybe it's within the context of a large family. Maybe it's in the classroom. The one who's the favorite usually likes the coveted spot while the others feel excluded. While the Father loves all His children, He's searching to and fro for those He can bless in a mighty way if their hearts are committed to Him. If you are an obedient child of the Most High, He considers you a favorite and desires to favor you. His favor is His exceptional kindness, His special regard for and being set apart for His use. When you receive God's favor, you are distinguished.

And just how does God show favor? He delights in favoring those that heed His commands. And He lets us know if we seek Him and find Him, we'll obtain favor. *For whoever finds me finds life, And obtains favor from the Lord Proverbs 8:35.* Mother, each time your womb has held a baby, you've been shown great favor. *The angel went to her and said, "Greetings, you who are highly favored! The Lord is with you." Luke 1:28.* Husbands, when you found your wife, you obtained favor. *He who finds a wife finds what is good and receives favor from the LORD. Proverbs 18:22.* And the blessing of favor even serves as protection. *Surely, Lord, you bless the righteous; you surround them with your favor as with a shield. Psalm 5:12.*

Just picture it. You walk into a grand ballroom and make your way down the long center aisle to the head table. Seated and smiling radiantly is Jesus and immediately to His right you catch a glimpse of the place card. Your child's name is on it! Your child has been hand selected by the Master to fulfill a great purpose. And here at this banquet, Jesus will bestow His blessing on your child. Time and time again in the word of God we see Him show favor by way of blessing, grace, mercy and protection. And today, your child is the highly favored one.

So how does your child qualify for this preferential treatment? Encourage your children to seek God earnestly. He assures if we seek, we shall find. Teach your children that obedience to God is the expectation. For He says to obey is better than sacrifice (1 Samuel 15:22). Through your own testimony, teach your children to have faith. And finally, admonish them to continually seek wisdom. Wait, here's another. Even in heeding your instructions, they can receive favor. *My son, do not forget my teaching, but keep my commands in your heart, for they will prolong your life many years and bring you peace and prosperity. Let love and faithfulness never leave you; bind them around your neck, write them on the tablet of your heart. Then you will win favor and a good name in the sight of God and man. Proverbs 3:1-4* The Lord desires to dispense His favor. Our job is to train our children to position themselves to receive it.

FAVOR WITH MEN

To grow in favor with men is to develop relationally. You ever meet people that just don't work well with others? Well, growing in favor with man is the opposite of that. One of the basic tenets of our faith, love your neighbor, requires us to be in relationship with others. When your children demonstrate an acute awareness of interpersonal relationships they will draw favor with men. Your children will be looked to, will be highly esteemed in their circle of influence, will seem wise beyond their years, will be trusted to carry out tasks, and will stand out in a crowd. When your children live in a way that is pleasing to God, they can't help but stand out. People will recognize their "good home training" which we know is their God Home Training.

In shepherding my little flock, one of my consistent prayers is that my children will grow in wisdom and stature, in favor with God and with man. And wouldn't you know, God is faithful. I am saying this as a caution to know what you're asking for. Have you ever prayed for patience? An answer to that prayer may look like you being placed in some trying predicament so that your patience muscle is exercised. The same can be said here. As I prayed this for my children and it came to pass, I don't know if I was ready. Then I found myself wanting to backpedal. I even went so far as to secretly pray that a door would close for one of my children because I simply couldn't foresee the family taking on another project. But sure enough, my child was selected. When I asked, "Why Lord? You know I can't handle another thing!" He answered, "You remember what you asked, that they grow in wisdom and stature, in favor with me and with man. I heard. I answered. I will not renege on my promise". Each and every day, they are growing wiser and standing taller.

PRACTICAL APPLICATION

Arrange an opportunity this week for your child to have a conversation with an older person (neighbor, grandparent, etc). Have your child ask what life was like when he/she was a child. Wisdom is gained under the tutelage of the wise. Also, plan and cook a meal together this week. Resist the urge to take over in the kitchen. Based on your child's age, let them do as much as possible.

prayer

Lord, thank you for being a good, good Father and walking alongside me as I mature in my own faith. It seems as if my children are growing by leaps and bounds. Show me how to maximize the time I have with them so that it is most fruitful. I repent for time and energy that has been spent on things that will not impact eternity. But I give thanks that you restore the years the swarming locusts have eaten. Let me take my own faith seriously and be diligent in seeking, praying and serving so that I am leading by example. I will be purpose driven in nurturing my children as they grow in faith, in wisdom, and in stature. I thank you that my children will flourish and reach their full potential in you.

⤳

Chapter 10

A FUTURE AND A HOPE

⤙

THE JOB OF THE CHRISTIAN parent is to point their children to the cross. God desires for His blessings to be passed on from generation to generation. *"In your seed all the nations of the earth shall be blessed, because you have obeyed My voice." Genesis 22:18* As you have journeyed through this entire book, we have been positioning our children to walk with God. My prayer is that your child and mine will seek to have a relationship with the Father for themselves, that they will walk in paths of righteousness for His namesake and that they will uncover their purpose and fulfill their destiny. As parents, we plant the seeds; along their journey, another waters but it is God that gives the increase. Because for all our preschool bible lessons, teen devotionals, vacation bible schools, Christian school and daily prayers, they

202 - PURPOSEFUL PARENTING

will still have to choose Christ for themselves. The work we have done has equipped them to choose well but the choice is still theirs to make.

While I am reminding you that the choice is theirs to make, that should not leave you concerned or worried. In fact, it should make you all the more hopeful. Once you have done your part in knowing the way, going the way and showing the way, the rest is in God's hands and in His hands your children will be established. It is His desire that not one should perish (2 Peter 3:9) and that includes your children. He simply wants you to do what He's called you to do in shepherding them and He'll take it from there. He will bring about what He has spoken. *"For I have chosen him, so that he will direct his children and his household after him to keep the way of the Lord by doing what is right and just, so that the Lord will bring about for Abraham what he has promised him." Genesis 18:19*

Part of your showing the way is to leave a godly legacy. This legacy is not a trail of crumbs that can be quickly snatched up and devoured by birds but is instead a rich heritage of faith marked with evidence that God's sovereign hand has been operating in our lives. *"Let this be written for a future generation, that a people not yet created may praise the Lord." Psalm 102:18* How are you helping your children see God's hand at work? In your everyday observations like birds in flight, a breeze or leaves changing color, they are all tangible evidence of God's wondrous works. When someone is healed, protected from calamity or shown divine favor, these are excellent opportunities to highlight His presence.

Through writing letters, journals, a blog, scrapbooking or even writing a book, you can leave a written record of faith to serve as a witness for the generations to come.

In *The Resolution for Women*, Priscilla Shirer shares, *"Our legacy of faith, compassion, gratitude, perseverance, forgiveness, patience, and love should be carefully crafted and then purposefully passed on as well. Things that aren't earned by shrewd investing but by simply living. Gifts that aren't reserved for major holidays and dressy events but are given out on Tuesdays and Saturday mornings, in your sweatpants, without a lot of fanfare and fireworks."*[1] She goes on to cite my favorite—Deuteronomy 30:19. The small decisions we make in our every day living amount to the legacy we are leaving for our children. When we look back over our years, I don't think we'll recount who did or did not brush their teeth. I don't think it'll matter if our children wore the latest fashions. What will matter is how earnestly we demonstrated love in a way that could be seen and felt. You may have been helped or harmed by the family legacy that was passed on to you. In showing the way, let love be the footprint you leave behind.

WIIFM

When you've left a legacy rich in love, love for your children and love for Christ, what's in it for them? Your children will be heirs to a bountiful inheritance. Isn't that what we desire, for our children to be the heirs of eternal life? I don't want my children to "adopt" my religion because it's comfortable or familiar. I don't want them to adopt it merely because I said so. While those reasons may have them living a Christian lifestyle, that won't secure a place for them in heaven. My prayer is that they will lay hold of what they've been taught and accept Christ for themselves. *But as for you, continue in what you have learned and have firmly believed, knowing from whom you learned it and how from childhood you have been acquainted with the sacred writings, which are able to make you wise for salvation through faith in Christ Jesus. All Scripture is breathed out by God and profitable for teaching, for reproof, for correction, and for training in righteousness, that the man of God may be competent, equipped for every good work. 2 Timothy 3:14-17*

Your child may think, yeah; that's great. That method worked for you. What's in it for me (WIIFM)? Well, what's in it for them is the security of everlasting life. Your children shall be recipients of Christ's unconditional love and that's something no one else in this world can give. They can be free from anxieties and addictions, and so many other problems that seem to plague young people. When they do things God's way, they receive the benefits of that relationship. Those benefits are God's abounding love, peace and favor.

FUTURE AND HOPE

Our children must walk the individual paths God's already preordained for them. As parents, we often try to contrive the plans we desire for them. And it can be devastating when our children don't "live up" to our grand plans. Yes, you may have visualized your daughter's name engraved on her lab coat but she may have it engraved on a smock instead as she gleefully plays with three-year olds all day as a daycare provider. It can also be equally crushing when we feel our children aren't living up to their God-given potential. Your children may live out many mountaintop and valley experiences. They may spend some years like the Israelites wandering in the wilderness. But no matter how circuitous their paths in life, the Lord's guiding hand will see them to their destiny.

> *For thus says the LORD: After seventy years are completed at Babylon, I will visit you and perform My good word toward you, and cause you to return to this place. For I know the thoughts that I think toward you, says the LORD, thoughts of peace and not of evil, to give you a future and a hope. Then you will call upon Me and go and pray to Me, and I will listen to you. Jeremiah 29:10-12*

No one wants his or her child to be wayward. Inasmuch as we don't want it, it is still a very present possibility. If we're completely honest with ourselves, it can easily happen to your child or mine. Heck, even you and I may have been the wayward one. It is not my intent to speak of negative possibility because we know love hopes for the best and believes the best. I'm just speaking from experience and observation that even in the most God-fearing Christian homes all are prone to fall into sin. But the hope we have rests in Christ. Even when the prodigal son fell into riotous living, redemption was made available. He was warmly received by his father and was restored.

Oh, how difficult it is to watch your children suffer. I have a friend who says children have your heart. The first few times I heard her say it, I didn't really understand what she meant. But through experience, I came to know what she was talking about. How it tore at my heart when one of my children was bullied at school and I felt like I wanted to get revenge. How my heart was rent in two when I was raising my sister and she wanted to blaze a different path than the one I thought she should pursue. How about when a child goes wayward and behaves in a way completely contrary to how you raised them? Or how about when you can't protect your child from an illness? Indeed, they have your heart.

If you are not careful, it can get such that you look to your children to fill your emotional love tank or you can attach their performance to your own status. It is folly for us to attach our personal measure of success to our children's achievement or lack thereof. It is a tremendous burden to place on a child in looking to them for love and validation as a parent. For all our best efforts to rear and disciple our children, they don't belong to us. They are with us for just a short period of impartation; then they are off to pursue the purposes and plans God has ordained for them. And at the appointed time, they will need to be released so they can live out their *future and hope*.

As you slowly release the reins, be encouraged. Even for the child taking the scenic route, there is hope. The scenic route provides many opportunities for character building. Behold; the beauty of the tough times knowing God causes all things to work together for the good. Poet Langston Hughes writes in Mother to Son, *"Well, son, I'll tell you: Life for me ain't been no crystal stair. It's had tacks in it, And splinters, And boards torn up, And places with no carpet on the floor—Bare. But all the time I'se been a-climbin' on"*[2] This truth is not relative just for today. In the bible, God gives us portraits of many lives that have taken the circuitous path. No matter how many loops and turns, the Lord's guiding hand saw them to their destiny and the same is true for your child and for mine. Let's look at these illuminating examples.

Moses

He was shipped downriver to avoid execution. He was found by Pharaoh's daughter, watched over by his sister and then reconnected with his own mother who nursed and cared for him. He was raised with access and wealth but left that for a life of uncertainty after witnessing the atrocities committed against his people, yet, he directly heard the voice of God. He was given a special mission by the Lord to free God's chosen people.

While he had difficulty speaking in public, he was placed in a position of prominence to directly confront Pharaoh. He saw the children of Israel through their wandering. And he led the people right to Canaan, just before they entered the Promised Land.

Joseph

He was his father's favorite. He was despised by his brothers and sold into slavery. Potiphar's wife claimed he tried to rape her and he was placed in prison. When in prison, he asked one of his fellow prisoners who was to be released to remember him but he was forgotten. Eventually, he was redeemed and exalted to the second in command only under Pharaoh. Under his leadership, the Egyptians did not die of hunger. He reconciled with his brothers and was reunited with his father. He was blessed to be a blessing.

David

Though he was a lowly shepherd boy, he was courageous. He killed a lion. He slew a giant. When the search commenced for the one to be anointed king, he was the last to be presented before the man of God, yet, he was the chosen one. He was both loved and hated by King Saul so much so that the king nearly killed him. He was an adulterer and a murderer. Even with his sin, he was still called a friend of God and through his lineage we would receive Christ the Messiah.

Saul (Paul)

Saul was a zealous Pharisee. He led the execution of believers and stood by and supported the murder of the first martyr, Stephen. Yet, he had an encounter with the Lord on Damascus Road. He was embraced by loving believers (James, Peter &

Barnabas). Though he was threatened, beaten, and imprisoned, he continued to witness. His writings comprise most of the New Testament. Through his written testimony, we are compelled to live faithfully and to serve others.

WHEN ALL HOPE IS LOST

Are you a parent who feels all hope is lost? As a parent, I often wonder what more I can do for my children. In all of our talking, advising, teaching, training, coaching, molding and shaping, there comes a point when even all our best efforts are just that; EFFORTS. The ONE sure thing we can do is pray. As I type these words, I'm sitting in a coffee shop. The woman opposite me is on her cell phone crying as she relays to the person listening that her daughter is fighting for her life. This mom is in a fight with the insurance company to pay for a costly drug that could potentially save the child's life. My heart bleeds for this mother who is doing all she can to save her daughter's life. She makes several other calls, seemingly all to no avail.

What more can this mother do? When all hope seems gone. When life and death hang in the balance. There always is and will always be prayer. Prayer is not our last resort but our first choice. Prayer is not our defensive strategy but our offensive stance. Praying for the big things and praying for the little things. Praying in the morning and praying in the evening, let us find ourselves in a perpetual state of prayer, interceding for our children.

Your prayers for your children will minister from heaven for generations to come. When you pray God's promises over your children, they are received at the throne of grace. And the assurance we have is that when we pray, He hears. And not only does He hear, He answers. When He answers, favor and blessing are released. Oh, that just ticks the enemy off for he knows the great and magnificent future and hope your child has. So, he and his imps get busy at trying to hold up and intercept your prayers. This is the point at which you may be discouraged. Hold fast to your confessions. Thank God for hearing and answering. "SEE" the prayers manifested in the lives of your children. And continue to stand, having done all to stand, rooted in the confidence that God's kingdom come, His will be done.

Prayer is the single most effective thing you can ever do as a parent. If you remember only one thing from this entire book, let it be this; when you are dead and gone, your prayers for your children will live on, so pray bold, effectual fervent prayers for your children with the absolute conviction that God is not a man that He should lie; thus, your prayers will be answered. Oh, the confidence in knowing that your prayers are drawing your children one step closer to Christ. Your prayers are igniting their fire to want to know Jesus for themselves. Your prayers are guiding them in paths of righteousness. Your prayers are keeping them safe. Your prayers are helping them have discernment. Their purpose is revealed and their destiny is manifesting all because of your prayers.

For all our trying to keep them safe, feed them right, manage their education, share our faith, all these are good, but pale in comparison to the power of our effectual fervent prayer. Our prayers have power. Our prayers have dunamis! Dunamis is a Greek word that loosely translates to strength, might, power or ability. It's where we get English words like dynamic and dynamite. Yes, God's dunamis is released when you pray. When you come to God on behalf of your children, praying prayers filled with His word, He is CERTAIN to deliver releasing His dunamis to affect their lives. And how do I know?

God gives confirmation. Hannah was a woman of prayer. She cried out to the Lord for a son. He heard her cry and blessed her and the child. Her son Samuel became a prophet at a young age. Mary was a woman of prayer. She kept the word in her heart and pondered on it. Aaron, the first High Priest carried the names of the children of Israel on his breastplate. When he would go to minister before the Lord, he bore their names on his chest. He carried his people before the Lord in prayer. And parents, I'm charging you to do the same. I beseech you to pray continually. Pray without ceasing. Never stop praying.

"Arise, cry out in the night, at the beginning of the night watches! Pour out your heart like water before the presence of the Lord! Lift your hands to him for the lives of your children, who faint for hunger at the head of every street." Lamentations 2:19

Parents, you don't like something you see in your child, stop badgering the child about it and take it to God in prayer. Do less talking to your child and more talking to God about your child. Call those things that are not as though they are. Have you got a child who is slothful? No need to attack the child. No need to call the child lazy. Take it directly to God in prayer. A targeted prayer might sound a little like this, "Lord I thank you that (child's name) has a mind to work heartily as unto you not unto man. I thank you that he will use his time, energy and efforts to bring you glory. He will not be like the sluggard with nothing to reap at harvest time, but will sow in due season to reap a bountiful harvest. Because he is diligent, his soul is richly supplied."

Indeed, this is our demonstration of the confidence that we can have in Christ. When we ask, be it according to His will, it shall be done for us and for our children. And because this prayer was based directly on His word, we KNOW He is faithful to do it. But let us be reminded that God will do it in the manner in which He chooses to do it. That may look a little different than what you had in mind. Parents, don't be discouraged when you've prayed and feel the answer isn't manifesting. It may just look different than you anticipated.

Let's face it; some days, you may wonder if all your work and praying has been in vain. Some days you may examine your children's behavior and choices and wonder, "Where did I go wrong?" Some days, you may feel as if all hope has been lost. Friend, I implore you to not lose hope. A shameful, weak tactic of the enemy is to try to make you believe all hope is gone. That is so far from the truth. Our hope is in Christ and He does not disappoint.

You are to stand firm on the battlefield, ready for war. But you will not fight this fight by waging war against your child. You will not berate, nag or pester your child about what they aren't doing, about how you didn't raise them this way, about all the many things they aren't doing. You will battle for your children on your knees. Remember, prayer is your strategy. Not merely complaining to God about what's not going right with your child, because frankly He already sees it. But you will declare the promises that God has said to you about your child.

What do you do when your child is in trouble? You cry out to God, just like the woman whose child was demon-possessed (Matthew 15). Initially, Jesus did not answer her. Then the disciples tried to shoo her away. But when you are crying out for your child, don't give up. Even when the naysayers are pushing you away like the disciples did, don't give up. Your naysayers may be family members, doctors, or even your own negative self-talk. When Jesus did finally acknowledge that mother, it was just for Him to clarify why He was there and it wasn't to meet her immediate need. While He may be in the area blessing your neighbor's child, don't give up. Just like blind Bartimaeus knew healing was in the vicinity, he remained hopeful. When you're standing in the presence of hope and healing, keep standing. She petitioned again, and again wasn't given a clear yes but it wasn't a NO either. So, this mama remained hopeful and would willingly accept a crumb of a blessing from the Master's hand because she KNEW it would be more than enough. In knowing that a crumb was enough, He blessed her radical faith.

Some days, you may just feel you want to curl up in a ball and just cry your eyes out. You may not have it in you to pray. You may be too upset or too hurt to even get yourself together. Can I give you a little encouragement for those days? Even on those days, God will see, He will hear and He will answer because of His love for you and for your children. Remember Hagar? She was the mom we talked about earlier who called Him the God Who Sees. When Hagar and Ishmael were cast out of Abraham's house and their food and water had been depleted, Hagar resigned that she and her son would die in the wilderness. She just sat there and cried. But the word says God heard the voice of the *lad*! When God heard the voice of the lad, the angel of God responded to *Hagar* from heaven with a word of comfort and confirmation. In that encounter, God also made provision for their survival (Genesis 21). Parents, don't lose hope, God sees, He hears and He answers. I keep saying this because I want you to grab hold of this powerful truth.

Mama, do you have a child you've been interceding for for years and you haven't seen a turnaround? Grandma, do you have a grandson that you need God to rescue? Teacher, do you have a student you are standing in the gap for? Dad, are you on your knees for your child? Let me say it again. Don't lose hope! Keep on fasting; keep praying, keep on believing because God is sure to perform it. He is not a man that he should lie. His word does not return void. He is a promise-keeping God. Your children just need you to advocate for them in prayer. The enemy will try to intervene but God will clear the path and give

ease of access. You have come boldly before the throne of grace
to obtain favor and He will grant it.

And how do I know your prayers will come to pass? I know
because:

- He is the God who sees (Genesis 16:13)
- He is the God who hears (1 John 5:14-15)
- He is the God who answers (Isaiah 65:24)
- He is not a man that He should lie (Numbers 23:19)
- His word does not return void (Isaiah 55:11)
- He is faithful to perform (Jeremiah 1:12)

You and your children are heirs to great blessing. Your children will live lives that bring glory and honor to God. They will
live lives that you will be proud of.

*"I have no greater joy than to hear that my children walk
in truth." 3 John 1:4*

Yet, even before you see the full manifestation of all that God
has promised, you can get a praise on your lips. Even before
Jesus and John grew up, Mary and Zechariah praised the Lord.

Mary's Song Luke 1:46-55
And Mary said:
"My soul glorifies the Lord
and my spirit rejoices in God my Savior,

for he has been mindful
of the humble state of his servant.
From now on all generations will call me blessed,
for the Mighty One has done great things for me—
holy is his name.
His mercy extends to those who fear him,
from generation to generation.
He has performed mighty deeds with his arm;
he has scattered those who are proud in their inmost thoughts.
He has brought down rulers from their thrones
but has lifted up the humble.
He has filled the hungry with good things
but has sent the rich away empty.
He has helped his servant Israel,
remembering to be merciful
to Abraham and his descendants forever,
just as he promised our ancestors."

Zechariah's Song Luke 1:67-79

His father Zechariah was filled with the Holy Spirit and prophesied:
"Praise be to the Lord, the God of Israel,
because he has come to his people and redeemed them.
He has raised up a horn of salvation for us
in the house of his servant David
(as he said through his holy prophets of long ago),
salvation from our enemies
and from the hand of all who hate us—

to show mercy to our ancestors
and to remember his holy covenant,
the oath he swore to our father Abraham:
to rescue us from the hand of our enemies,
and to enable us to serve him without fear
in holiness and righteousness before him all our days.
And you, my child, will be called a prophet of the Most High;
for you will go on before the Lord to prepare the way for him,
to give his people the knowledge of salvation
through the forgiveness of their sins,
because of the tender mercy of our God,
by which the rising sun will come to us from heaven
to shine on those living in darkness
and in the shadow of death,
to guide our feet into the path of peace."

In case you still have a sliver of doubt, let's examine a few more figures that took what seemed an indirect path yet are walking in greatness.

Techie, business mogul, and philanthropist, Bill Gates had great promise. At a young age, he demonstrated brilliance. He went on to attend Harvard University but dropped out of school to pursue starting his own business. While that was a very risky move, it led to him co-founding Microsoft Corporation. I would venture to think his parents, a prominent lawyer and a board of directors' member, would have been taken aback by his decision to drop out but it proved a successful move in the end.

Author, TV & Radio host, former politician and prolific motivational speaker, Les Brown stands today encouraging others to follow their dreams. And he knows from personal experience that it's possible to achieve greatness even from humble beginnings. He was given up for adoption then adopted and raised by a cafeteria worker. He was labeled retarded in grade school and had low self-esteem. With hard work and determination, he went from being a sanitation worker to motivating the masses.

And even my own uncle-in-law. As a child, he was a stutterer and was in Special Education classes. Because of his stuttering, he was encouraged to adopt a trade. Being a hard worker and keen observer, he was introduced to shoe repair by his big brother, James. Today, my uncle John "Peterbug" Matthews is a well-respected community leader on affluent Capitol Hill in Washington, D.C. In addition to being an instructor, he runs Peter Bug Shoe Repair Academy, where he has been mending shoes and hearts since 1977. And in 2013, the street in front of his shoe repair shop was officially named Peterbug Matthews Way.

Like a 5000-piece mosaic puzzle, the Lord knows each and every piece. He knows how each piece is cut and where it belongs. He is the only one with the completed picture in mind. In the end, it is Him who lays all the pieces out, flips them over, and puts them into place. So, give a shout of praise for the God who knows, the God who sees and the God who puts it all together. Praise Him because your children are in His hands and strategically, He's working all things together for their good.

PRACTICAL APPLICATION

If you are a Believer, share with your child your conversion experience, including the events that led up to you accepting Christ. Remember, we overcome by the blood of the Lamb and the word of the testimony. Your Christian experience testimony will resonate deeply with your children.

If you have not accepted Jesus as personal Lord and Savior, I invite you to find out more about Him. Make plans to attend church with your child THIS coming Sunday. Perhaps a co-worker has invited you and you can finally take them up on the offer. Or maybe you've been driving past a church for years and thought about stopping in but never did. There's no time like the present.

prayer

Lord, despite my best parenting efforts, I realize that I am not my child's Holy Spirit. Please forgive me for when I have stepped out of line and tried to assume your role. Lord, I know that my children are in your strong, capable hands. I trust your sovereignty to see them through to the future and hope you've secured for them. On days when it seems as if all hope is lost, I will remember your promises and remain steadfast in prayer. I rest in the hope that you don't want even one to perish including my child. So, continue to draw them to yourself until they accept your invitation for salvation. In you, their future looks bright indeed.

⤳

Chapter 11

NOW WHAT?

⌁

ROOM TO GROW

Given the right conditions, your children have the ability to grow and prosper exponentially. But their ability to do so is directly contingent upon their conditions. With that said, are you providing conditions conducive to growth? My grandmother had a green thumb. In her historic Back Bay apartment was a window that dished up a feast for the eyes. Gazing out, I could see the "Pru", Copley Square, The John Hancock Building, and Christian Science Plaza, all iconic peaks in the Boston skyline. But most immediate, that window and its adjoining corners held at times nearly 50 plants. Big ones and small ones, cacti and dieffenbachia, little lemon plants and terrariums, they were all nurtured under her loving hand. Needless to say, I have a black thumb and even killed the cilantro I was trying to grow, but one valuable lesson I learned from her was pot size matters. I can vividly recall going to the hardware store beneath her apartment to get bags of potting soil. She stressed the importance of the plants being in the right sized pots. She showed me how dense, tight and restricted the root system got when in a pot too small.

What happens then to our children when they aren't given room to be themselves? We micromanage every facet of their lives. We choke out room for individual expression. Their growth is stifled. Our children aren't given room to be themselves and grow into the persons God created them to be. Perhaps you are "shaping" them to be just like you and to only live up to your expectations. No room is extended to explore their interests or to maximize their natural strengths and abilities. Parents, I'm not saying this to point fingers at you. I'm pointing this out so you don't miss an opportunity to nurture their gifts.

We don't want our children to live life wondering "What if...." As a child, my husband was a gifted artist. He could easily replicate any Marvel superhero with ease. Right down to the sculpted abs, my husband would spend hours daydreaming and drawing. But the gift was never cultivated. At times, he's wondered what would have happened if he'd been afforded an opportunity to pursue art. My father always wanted to pursue music. My grandfather, a strict old-fashioned man from the British West Indies was not going to have his son dabbling in music. So out went my father's dreams to pursue music. Fortunately, in his adulthood, my father exercised his right to pursue his passion. He even built a state of the art music studio inside his home. But I wonder what would have happened if my grandfather had fostered my dad's love of music. Parents, let us not be the reason our children have to wonder, "what if".

Just like trees planted by rivers of living water, our children will bear fruit, their leaves will not wither and whatever godly pursuits they have will prosper (Psalm 1). Trees planted in fertile soil don't need to be messed with too much. The same can be said for your children. While planted firmly in your home, under your values in a soil that is rich in the nutrient love, they will thrive.

Have you ever seen a bonsai tree? I am fortunate to be able to visit the U.S. National Arboretum regularly. Housed there is the National Bonsai and Penjing Museum, which holds one of the largest bonsai collections in North America. Bonsai is the Japanese art form of growing miniature trees in containers. Bonsai trees themselves are not grown from miniature tree seeds but from standard size tree seeds. The branches are cultivated to remain small. The artisan carefully trims, prunes, cuts roots, and restricts pot size in order to craft these beautiful little works of art.

Contrasting with their tiny scale is the baobab tree. The baobab is a prehistoric tree dating to 200 million years ago. In Africa, it is a symbol of life and positivity. It adapts well to its environment. In the rainy season, it absorbs and stores water to preserve it for the dry season to come. There are trees still around that have been carbon dated to nearly 6,000 years old.

The baobab can grow almost 100 feet tall with a trunk up to 36 feet wide! They even provide shelter, food and water for humans and animals.

The baobab, unlike the bonsai, has been provided optimal conditions to grow. What kind of conditions are you providing for your children's growth? Give your children space; space to try things and space to be creative. Is every moment a planned, carefully calculated educational experience? Or do they have room to play and get dirty? I, myself, have been guilty of squeezing out organic learning experiences. I, too, have filled many hours of my children's days with well-meaning busyness. As I mentioned in a previous chapter, one summer we tried something different. I told the children we would not do business as usual. Out was ripping and running in a million different directions for camps, museums, and shows; instead, in would be relaxing days at home. You know what? My first-born told me at the conclusion that it was the best summer ever.

Let's set our intentions on raising baobabs not bonsais. While the bonsai has been skillfully wrought and is a beauty to admire, it's been cut, clipped and contained. Your children are baobabs. And like the baobab, affectionately known as the tree of life, your children, in an otherwise arid and dry land, will grow and prosper. Your children will be able to withstand the elements. Your children will be filled from within with water that will nourish their souls. Say it with me, "My child is a baobab NOT a bonsai!" When you look upon them, see them as trees of life.

DOING IT RIGHT

So, are we doing it right? Who knows. What I've found along this journey is that most of the parenting being done is being done to me. God has taken out a heart of stone and given me a heart of flesh (Ezekiel 36:26). Gone is the woman who was highly critical of others who arrived late. In is the woman who's had a diaper blow out right when headed out the door. Gone is the woman who made judgments based on how neat and put together the children look. In is the woman who embraces the joy in the child's eyes as they dance on the playground in their pajamas. More empathetic, more compassionate, and exponentially more patient is the fruit born from this parenting journey. Honoring my temple, rest, exercise and unconditional love were learned directly through the act of parenting. Yup; I'm the one that's done the most changing around here.

> *"To be a good father and mother requires that the parents defer many of their own needs and desires in favor of the needs of their children. As a consequence of this sacrifice, conscientious parents develop a nobility of character and learn to put into practice the selfless truths taught by the Savior Himself." James E. Faust*

In our own strength, we can only parent to the extent to which we have been parented. We can only give love in a way that is familiar to us. We can only give what we know which is why it's crucial to abide in Jesus. Staying connected to the vine is the only way we can render true love. He downloads love directly from His heart to ours then we, in turn, release that love out onto our children. Remember you are a conduit not a cul-de-sac of love. The love emanates from Christ, flows through you then out onto your children who will, in turn, flow it to others.

But what happens when you have some cracks in your own heart? Perhaps there are some broken places that need mending. As mentioned at the start of this book, you have to be made whole. Ask God to reveal any brokenness in your own life. It was through parenting that my own issues rose to the surface. I had such deep pain from not having been mothered. My own mother's personal struggles with alcohol and drug addiction left her incapable of being there for me. As I progressed through my adult years, I thought I was okay but it was in having my own children that the magnitude of that void became apparent. My cracks caused me to be an overly protective and overly harsh parent.

Though I couldn't identify it immediately, I knew something was "off" in my parenting. I asked God to show me what the issue was. And sure enough, He began by taking me back to my childhood, exposing the fractured little me. As I cried and prayed, His love flooded those areas and mended my broken places. For me, it was not a quick process and I prayed for my children to be covered as I healed. Gradually, I've learned to work through my own issues so that I can parent my children based on who they are and what they need. Not every day is perfect but I feel I'm headed in the right direction.

Growing up, I rarely went to church but one thing I remember is a hymn called, "Yield Not to Temptation." I attended a week-long revival with a family friend and the children were required to memorize a hymn. I recall selecting that particular hymn because it was shorter and easier to memorize. One of the lines from the hymn is "each victory will help you some other to win". In parenting, you will have successes and you will have what seem like setbacks. Please don't magnify the setbacks. Be strengthened knowing each parenting victory fortifies you to win another and another.

Let me also encourage you to embrace the experiences you've gone through—the good, the bad and the ugly. Be grateful for all your experiences, as they've directly impacted the person you are today. Do not begrudge any part of your story. Did you grow up in a single parent home? Did you grow up wearing hand me downs? Did you grow up feeling like the ugly duckling? Is your story that you did NOT have hard times but lived a good life and because of that feel your story is boring? Whatever your story, embrace it. And not only embrace it, but share it with your children. You've been commanded to tell your story to your children (Psalm 78). Your story, which is part of their story, is more fascinating than anything they could ever watch on TV. Your story directly shows your children God's love and grace in action.

OPERATING UNDER GRACE

Recently at church, two people made reference to me being superwoman. Perhaps they've seen me active in ministry, caring for this little flock of six and think I've got super powers. So, for once and for all, let me dispel this myth. I am no superwoman; more like super mistake maker, super grace receiver, super Jesus girl. Truth be told, I am vulnerable. I do get tired. I, too, have my kryptonite. If they only saw me when the pot of rice was on the stove burning, holding a crying baby on the hip, trying to help four with homework and emailing the teacher about a missing assignment all at the same time, they would see my fragility. But God! Aaron Shust sums it up well for me singing, *"My Savior loves, my Savior lives, My Savior's always there for me. My God He was, my God He is, my God He's always gonna be".*

Without my Jesus, I am nothing. Apart from the vine, we are nothing.

"I am the vine, you are the branches. He who abides in Me, and I in him, bears much fruit; for without Me you can do nothing." John 15:5

That's as super as it gets. We should all strive to be super vine clingers. Have you ever tried to be Superman or Superwoman? Have you ever tried to do and be everything to everybody? How'd that work out for ya? I don't know about you, but that left me depleted. You can only love through Christ who strengthens you. You can only give through Christ who strengthens you. You can only serve through Christ who strengthens you.

Be aware so that you don't fall into the trap of trying to be the perfect parent. There is no such thing. You don't have to try to do all and be all. Neither do your children. Don't throw them into the rat race early of trying to do all and be all. Stay in your lane and be proficient at what God's called you to do. He's given YOU a specific assignment so stick to it. It's when you go picking up other things and your hands get too full that you can get into trouble.

Let me give you an example. God has given me the ability to do hair. I've had repeated requests for styling. I've even had a stylist see my work and give me some pointers on booking clients. But God told me, "This gift is for HOUSEHOLD USE ONLY". I briefly entertained the thought of earning that money. Yes, I could do a few heads on the weekend. Then came the gentle shoulder tap, "FOR HOUSEHOLD USE ONLY." Thus, I quickly extinguished the idea because I want to operate in his perfect will, not His permissive will. I also make body butter. I've had repeated requests to make it in big batches. I've had people offer to purchase it. But again, I decline because I don't want to misappropriate my grace.

I invite you to join me in clinging fiercely to the Father. From this place, you don't have to worry about perfection but will be the recipient of grace. Do you ever feel unqualified, inadequate, weak or incapable in your role as a parent? Sometimes I do. Sometimes I wonder if all my parenting efforts will pay off. But the wondering is usually a trick of the enemy. When he sees a crack in your finish, he attempts to seep his poison in. He'll try to play on your weaknesses and parenting is an area in life where we can feel most weak. Remember, your children have your heart and that makes you vulnerable. But with the Lord, vulnerability is okay. *But he said to me, "My grace is sufficient for you, for my power is made perfect in weakness." Therefore I will boast all the more gladly about my weaknesses, so that Christ's power may rest on me. That is why, for Christ's sake, I delight in weaknesses, in insults, in hardships, in persecutions, in difficulties. For when I am weak, then I am strong.* 2 Corinthians 12:9-10 Not only are you made strong when you are weak, but God wants to use you right in that place of weakness.

When people see me with my children and say things like "Motherhood is your ministry", my flesh used to prickle because the voice of the accuser said, "Yeah, but they didn't see you roll your eyes at your kid last night". But I know the truth. I KNOW that the Lord has supernaturally taught me to love, nurture and shepherd this little flock. I know He's using me right in the place where I feel weak.

How about you? As a parent, do you ever feel weak or incapable? If the answer is yes, then we are in good company. Just like He used Moses. Doubting Moses. Unqualified Moses. Fearful Moses. Moses who was fearful and ran from his staff when it turned into a snake; God told him to PICK UP that very thing and use it as a sign. The same thing that Moses ran from was the very instrument that would hit a rock to bring water to nourish the people and would part the waters so they could cross on dry land. God was purposeful and intentional in sending those little people into your life. God used Moses' weakness and He wants to use yours too.

Your weaknesses aren't flaws that need to be magnified but are opportunities for God's grace to be glorified. Please do not condemn yourself when you make parenting mistakes. Identify the voice of condemnation. Is that negative self-chatter even your voice or the voice of the accuser? The voice may be a critical boss you had or a disapproving relative. Let the accuser be cast down (Revelation 12:10). Cancel that voice and hearken to the True Voice. God's voice is gentle and gracious. His voice convicts but it does not condemn.

Being weak and making mistakes are part of the human experience. Give yourself permission to experience a full range of emotions and partake in the depth and breadth of your personal experiences, including the messy parenting days. Parenting is by far not a perfect process. See the beauty in the mess-ups and take your eye off what you perceive to be errors and put your eye on Jesus. He is the best parent ever and loves you unconditionally. I count you courageous for even stepping up to the plate and being willing to take your turn at bat. You may not always hit a homerun, but you put on your uniform, took the long walk to plate, lifted your bat, and let it fly. Your arms may be weak, but in that very instance, HIS power is made perfect in your weakness.

To be compassionate is to care about the misfortune or suffering of others. But where is your self-compassion? I say you owe it to yourself. Be compassionate with yourself. The danger of being too harsh with you is that it can translate to being harsh with the children. If you are overly concerned with how others view your parenting, you can end up being harder on your child than necessary. Then you can become even harsher on yourself for having been harsh to the child when that wasn't even your original intent. This can be a painful cycle. So, as you extend compassion and grace to others, make sure you start with yourself.

FOR THE HARD DAYS

There is so much joy to be shared when engaging with children. Endless jokes, an eruption of giggles and effortless smiles abound when in their company. Inevitably though, there will be hard days; days when you are up at 3:00am cleaning up throw up, days when you are rocking an inconsolable child in your lap and days when you feel nothing is going right. On those days, you must remember grace. Remember, if He's called you to it, He's going to give you the grace to do it.

> *"And God is able to make all grace abound toward you, that you, always having all sufficiency in all things, may have an abundance for every good work." 2 Corinthians 9:8 NKJV*

This is a promise God is sure to keep. When we look at bible verses, we tend to see them in isolation but let's look at the verse 2 Corinthians 9:8 in its context. The verses that precede it talk about serving the Lord's people. They encourage us to give and to not only give but to give generously and to not only give generously but to do so cheerfully. So, as you are selflessly giving and serving your children, He WILL make all grace abound toward you.

There is a saying, "When the going gets tough, the tough get going." It generally means when we face hard times, we should work even harder to overcome. I say when facing difficult parenting days, don't try to work even harder. I say to literally STOP, breathe deeply, inhaling God's grace and breathe out releasing worry, doubt, frustration, etc. Try it with me now. Deep breath in…GRACE…release…

In the trying times, keep the end in mind. Remember we talked about maintaining an eternal perspective? I once had a ministry leader share something that's stuck with me for years. She was talking about maintaining joy in the home. She shared on joy robbers. And she encouraged us to ask ourselves; "Is it going to matter in five years? Is it going to matter in 10 years? Is it going to matter in eternity?" Those questions help me keep the "end in mind" perspective.

Another concept we discussed previously was embracing the now moment. When we embrace this very moment, we have an opportunity to still time and capture the now. This moment is then free to be itself without the influence of past experiences or future expectations. In THIS moment, you and your children are alive, are in a measure of health, have a measure of provision. Whatever the extenuating circumstances, beauty, majesty and splendor are yours to behold in this moment. A child's past actions can try to color how you view them right now but by embracing this moment, you free yourself and your child to not be held hostage to the past but to focus on what is. This moment is true reality so make it count.

When all is said and done, though you may have sprouted a gray hair or two, remember as my grandmother used to say, "And this too shall pass." Temper tantrums. This too shall pass. Lost homework. This too shall pass. Teenage meltdowns. This too shall pass.

READY TO FLY

So, at the end of the day, what was it all for? The countless hours of training, coaching, and teaching day after day were not merely for their personal benefit. Nor do we make the investment for our own gratification. Prayerfully, we made that investment in order that they may affect change in the world. Our children will be the next surgeons performing life-saving surgery. Our children will be the next generation of pastors, bringing the Gospel to the ends of the earth. One of our children will be the very one to solve the global food crisis. One of our children will discover how to supply people with clean drinking water.

You have been grooming and shaping your children so that they will lead fulfilled lives. Not only are their lives fulfilling, they are also purpose filled. Your children are productive citizens of this world and of the kingdom of God. Your children are arrows who will set forth in flight, out of your home to contend with enemies in this world (Psalm 127:3-4). Your children will help heal humanity. Your children will serve those among us that need the most help. The carbon footprint they will leave behind will be an imprint of love. Our world groans in pain and love is the answer to heal humanity. Through your consistent deposits of love, your children will be compelled to love God, themselves, and others. The most basic, yet essential, human need in life is love and your children are the embodiment of love.

No matter what brought you to this book, we are all here on purpose. That's just how God works. In our time together, we revisited God's plan and purpose for our children. We came to see that connecting with them begins by reaching their hearts. We reach the heart when we extend unconditional love and acceptance as we guide them through the various ages and stages of development. We learned that discipline and training is a lifelong process that is instrumental in shaping character. And character is the tool which allows our children to be in it to win it for Christ. All the while, they are growing wise and standing tall as they walk out the bright future and hope promised by the Lord.

....

PRACTICAL APPLICATION

As a student of your child, identify their strengths. Have you created opportunities for them to nurture their natural gifting and abilities? For the next two weeks, be intentional about providing opportunities for your children to use their gift. If your child is a natural speaker, create an opportunity for them to give a speech (even if family is the audience). If you've got a doodler or artist, give them a new set of art supplies or sign them up for an art class. If you've got a child that's naturally athletic, get out there WITH your child and play tennis, football or do some sprints. Purposeful and intentional exercising of their natural gifts is the plan for the next two weeks.

....

prayer

*Ever faithful, ever true, ever loving, that's what
you are God. You are the one who knows our
beginning from our end. Lord, for every step
of our journey, You have been there. From our
own experiences being parented to us parenting
today, You have witnessed everything. For the
days we've parented out of our brokenness, God
forgive us. Thank You for Your unending grace.
We thank You for filling our cracks so that we are
healthy and whole to offer unconditional love to
our children. Let us create environments conducive to their continued growth and not stifle their
individual expression. We know that they are
under our care for an appointed time. When it is
time for them to pursue their own path, we won't
be gripped by fear, but, in love, we will release
them back to You, knowing your sovereign hand
will continue to guide them. With our eyes set
on eternity, we thank You that we get to play an
instrumental role in building Your kingdom
here on earth.*

AFTERWORD

IT IS MY HOPE THAT the words shared here have inspired you to parent with purpose. I pray you've given the practical applications your best effort. If reading this book has caused you to become more aware of the behavior you're modeling, then I count it a tremendous success. If reading these pages has caused you to hug more, snuggle more, or listen to your children more attentively, you've made my day. If you've learned to "see" your child through the eyes of love and compassion, I'm doing the happy dance. Writing this book has certainly had a great impact on me as the Lord is holding me accountable for living out what He's revealed in these pages.

I'd love to join you as you continue your parenting journey. Won't you share your thoughts with me? We are in this together and we thrive when in a loving, supportive community. You can connect with me @ www.inspiredtolivefully.com

My personal prayer for this assignment is that my parenting emanates as a light, drawing my children and others closer to Christ.

ACKNOWLEDGEMENTS

TO MY BEST FRIEND, TOMAR, I'm so happy to be running the two-legged race of life with you. Out of our union, generations to come shall be blessed.

Sometimes you don't know what's in you until others help draw it out. I would like to thank Mrs. Jackie Parker for saying there was a need to talk about parenting and that I was the one to do it. I would like to thank Pastor John K. Jenkins, Sr. and First Lady Trina Jenkins of The First Baptist Church of Glenarden for their commitment to ensuring God's people are duly equipped with the Word. Additionally, I would like to thank Deaconess Angelette Featherstone for her gentle spirit, guidance and for whispering nearly eight years ago, that the *Raising Godly Children* focus study would be this book you're holding in your hands.

Finally, to my Dad, though our years living together were short, the time spent continues to reap a harvest in your grandchildren.

NOTES

Chapter 1 Introduction

1. *Juvenile Justice In A Developmental Framework*. Rep. Chicago: MacArthur Foundation, 2015. Web. 7 Oct. 2016.

Chapter 2 God's Plan and Purpose

1. "The Priorities, Challenges, and Trends in Youth Ministry." *Barna Group*. Barna Group, 6 Apr. 2016. Web. 30 Oct. 2016.

Chapter 3 Connecting with The Heart

1. Winfrey, Oprah, and Toni Morrison. "Oprah's Lifeclass, Does Your Face Light Up?" *Oprah's Lifeclass*. May 2000. Television.

2. Van Vliet, V. (2012). *Communication Model by Albert Mehrabian*. Retrieved 20 Oct. 2016 from ToolsHero: http://www.toolshero.com/communication-skills/communication-model-mehrabian/

Chapter 4 Love and Acceptance

1. Campbell, D. Ross, MD. *How To Really Love Your Child*. Colorado Springs: Cook Communications Ministries, 2003. Print.

2. "William Barclay Daily Study Bible Eph 4 Commentary." *StudyLight.org*. William Barclay Daily Study Bible, n.d. Web. 29 Sept. 2016.

Chapter 5 Ages and Stages
1. Swan, Monte, and David Biebel. *Romancing Your Child's Heart*. Sisters, Or.: Multnomah, 2002. 111. Print.

Chapter 6 Discipline and Training
1. "Character Case Studies." *Character*. N.p., n.d. Web. 28 Oct. 2016.

2. Hanna, Jason. "'Affluenza' Teen Tentatively Gets 2 Years." *CNN*. Cable News Network, 14 Apr. 2016. Web. 20 Sept. 2016.

Chapter 7 Character Development
1. Adapted from Lockett, Michael. "The Frog in the Milk Pail." The Frog in the Milk Pail. Dr. Michael Lockett, n.d. Web. 28 Sept. 2016.

2. Shirer, Priscilla Evans. "Loving My Children." *The Resolution: For Women*. Nashville, TN: B & H Pub. Group, 2011. 219. Print.

3. Brown, Brené. *Daring Greatly: How the Courage to Be Vulnerable Transforms the Way We Live, Love, Parent, and Lead*. New York, NY: Gotham, 2012. 86-99. 100 Print.

Chapter 8 Godly vs Worldly Parenting

1. The Barna Group. "The State of the Church 2016—Barna Group." *Barna Group*. The Barna Group, 15 Sept. 2016. Web. 29 Oct. 2016.

Chapter 9 Growing in Wisdom and Stature

1. Blessitt, Arthur. "Miles Jesus and Mary Walked." *The Official Website of Arthur Blessitt*. Arthur Blessitt, n.d. Web. 01 Nov. 2016.

Chapter 10 A Future and A Hope

1. Shirer, Priscilla Evans. "Leaving a Godly Legacy." *The Resolution: For Women*. Nashville, TN: B & H Pub. Group, 2011. 250. Print.

2. Hughes, Langston. "Mother to Son." *Poetry Foundation*. Poetry Foundation, n.d. Web. 08 Nov. 2016. Reprinted with the permission of Harold Ober Associates Incorporated

ABOUT THE AUTHOR

TYRA LANE-KINGSLAND IS NO STRANGER to inspiring the hearts of the masses. From her role as a Women's Ministry Leader to spending over five years as a performance improvement coach and facilitator for a Top Twenty Fortune 500 Company, Tyra has provided encouragement to countless people. Her desire is to help people experience living fully through delightful obedience to God, embracing the "now" moment and honoring the temple through proper nourishment, rest and exercise.

Having been recognized as a Competent Communicator with Toastmasters International, Tyra is a sough-after speaker. With a passion for writing and teaching, Tyra has written and facilitated classes on raising children and healthy living. She also holds a Bachelor's Degree in Journalism from Howard University.

Tyra is an attentive wife and mother to six children, ages thirteen and under. A resident of a Metropolitan Washington suburb, Tyra enjoys spending time encouraging others, reading, writing, cooking, and admiring the natural beauty surrounding her home. With a penchant for healthy eating, Tyra is always on the lookout for new, exciting recipes and can often be found showing others her kitchen best practices.

Having endured a tumultuous childhood but walking in victory today, Tyra knows first-hand that God trades beauty for ashes, joy for pain and a garment of praise for a spirit of heaviness. Knowing that God causes all things to work together for good, Tyra is eager to ignite an awareness of God's presence in everyday circumstances.

CPSIA information can be obtained
at www.ICGtesting.com
Printed in the USA
FSOW04n0949131217
41825FS

9 780997 833232